T0343433

ALSO IN THE *FOLGER GUIDE* SERIES

The Folger Guide to Teaching *Hamlet*

The Folger Guide to Teaching *Macbeth*

The Folger Guide to Teaching *Romeo and Juliet*

The Folger Guide to Teaching *A Midsummer Night's Dream*

The Folger Guide to Teaching *Othello*

The Folger Guides to Teaching Shakespeare Series
— Volume 5 —

Peggy O'Brien, Ph.D., General Editor

Folger Shakespeare Library
WASHINGTON, DC

Simon & Schuster Paperbacks
NEW YORK   AMSTERDAM/ANTWERP   LONDON
TORONTO   SYDNEY   NEW DELHI

Simon & Schuster
1230 Avenue of the Americas
New York, NY 10020

First Simon & Schuster trade paperback edition March 2025

SIMON & SCHUSTER PAPERBACKS and colophon are registered trademarks
of Simon & Schuster, LLC

For information about special discounts for bulk purchases,
please contact Simon & Schuster Special Sales at 1-866-506-1949
or business@simonandschuster.com.

The Simon & Schuster Speakers Bureau can bring authors
to your live event. For more information or to book an event, contact the
Simon & Schuster Speakers Bureau at 1-866-248-3049
or visit our website at www.simonspeakers.com.

Interior design by Paul Dippolito

Manufactured in the United States of America

1   3   5   7   9   10   8   6   4   2

Library of Congress Cataloging-in-Publication Data is available upon request.

ISBN 978-1-9821-0564-8
ISBN 978-1-6680-1762-3 (ebook)

THE FOLGER SHAKESPEARE LIBRARY

The Folger Shakespeare Library makes Shakespeare's stories and the world in which he lived accessible. Anchored by the world's largest Shakespeare collection, the Folger is a place where curiosity and creativity are embraced and conversation is always encouraged. Visitors to the Folger can choose how they want to experience the arts and humanities, from interactive exhibitions to captivating performances, and from pathbreaking research to transformative educational programming.

The Folger seeks to be a catalyst for:

Discovery. The Folger's collection is meant to be used, and it is made accessible in the Folger's Reading Room to anyone who is researching Shakespeare or the early modern world. The Folger collection has flourished since founders Henry and Emily Folger made their first rare book purchase in 1889, and today contains more than 300,000 objects. The Folger Institute facilitates scholarly and artistic collections- based research, providing research opportunities, lectures, conversations, and other programs to an international community of scholars.

Curiosity. The Folger designs learning opportunities for inquisitive minds at every stage of life, from tours to virtual and in-person workshops. Teachers working with the Folger are trained in the Folger Method, a way of teaching complex texts like Shakespeare that enables students to own and enjoy the process of close-reading, interrogating texts, discovering language with peers, and contributing to the ongoing human conversation about words and ideas.

Participation. The Folger evolves with each member and visitor interaction. Our exhibition halls, learning lab, gardens, theater, and historic spaces are open to be explored and to provide entry points for connecting with Shakespeare and the Folger's collection, as well as forming new pathways to experiencing and understanding the arts.

Creativity. The Folger invites everyone to tell their story and experience the stories of and inspired by Shakespeare. Folger Theatre, Music, and Poetry are programmed in conversation with Folger audiences, exploring our collective past, present, and future. Shakespeare's imagination resonates across centuries, and his works are a wellspring for the creativity that imbues the Folger's stage and all its programmatic offerings.

The Folger welcomes everyone—from communities throughout Washington, DC, to communities across the globe—to connect in their own way. Learn more at folger.edu.

IMAGE CREDITS

Morocco: Abd el-Ouahed ben Messaoud ben Mohammed Anoun, Moorish Ambassador to Queen Elizabeth I (1600).
©RESEARCH AND CULTURAL COLLECTIONS, UNIVERSITY OF BIRMINGHAM

Smith, John. The generall historie of Virginia, New-England, and the Summer Isles . . . (1631) map of Virginia after page 168.
CALL # STC 22790C.2. USED BY PERMISSION OF THE FOLGER SHAKESPEARE LIBRARY.

Hollar, Wenceslaus. Head of a Black woman with a lace kerchief hat (1645) no. 46, plate opposite page 88.
CALL # ART VOL. B35 NO.46. USED BY PERMISSION OF THE FOLGER SHAKESPEARE LIBRARY.

Hollar, Wenceslau. Head of a Black woman in profile to left (1645).
CALL # ART 237212. USED BY PERMISSION OF THE FOLGER SHAKESPEARE LIBRARY.

Hollar, Wenceslaus. Head of a young Black boy in profile to right (17th century).
CALL # ART 236023. USED BY PERMISSION OF THE FOLGER SHAKESPEARE LIBRARY.

Ira Aldridge's first appearance at Covent Gardens in the role of Othello—a play bill dated 1833 plus 2 small engraved portraits and an article in German, mounted together (early to mid-19th century).
CALL # ART FILE A365.5 NO.5. USED BY PERMISSION OF THE FOLGER SHAKESPEARE LIBRARY.

La tragedia de Romeo y Julieta. William Shakespeare; Pablo Neruda.
BUENOS AIRES, EDITORIAL LOSADA, S.A., 1964.

The tragedy of Othello, the Moor of Venice.
PROMPT OTH. FO.2, PP. 129–130, IMAGE 68005. USED BY PERMISSION OF THE FOLGER SHAKESPEARE LIBRARY.

The tragedy of Othello, the Moor of Venice.
PROMPT OTH. FO.2, PP. 129–130, IMAGE 7926. USED BY PERMISSION OF THE FOLGER SHAKESPEARE LIBRARY.

Napoleon Leading the Army over the Alps (2005). © Kehinde Wiley.
COURTESY SEAN KELLY GALLERY, NEW YORK.

Passing/Posing (Assumption) (2003).
© KEHINDE WILEY. COURTESY SEAN KELLY GALLERY, NEW YORK.

"Miss Susanna Gale" (2009).
© KEHINDE WILEY. COURTESY SEAN KELLY GALLERY, NEW YORK.

Passing/Posing (Female Prophet Deborah) (2003).
© KEHINDE WILEY. COURTESY SEAN KELLY GALLERY, NEW YORK.

Passing/Posing (Immaculate Consumption) (2003).
© KEHINDE WILEY. COURTESY SEAN KELLY GALLERY, NEW YORK.

Two pages from *L'organe des arts* (1852).
BILL BOX Z5 B9TR 1852 ITEMS 1–4, IMAGE 164898. USED BY PERMISSION OF THE FOLGER SHAKESPEARE LIBRARY.

Moblard, Victor. Mr. Grist as Othello (late 19th century).
ART BOX M785 NO.6, IMAGE 36246. USED BY PERMISSION OF THE FOLGER SHAKESPEARE LIBRARY.

Tenniel, John. Othello (1876).
ART BOX T311 NO.4, IMAGE 35320. USED BY PERMISSION OF THE FOLGER SHAKESPEARE LIBRARY.

Mr. G.V. Brooke as Othello (1850 to 1876).
ART FILE B872 NO.1, IMAGE 21242. USED BY PERMISSION OF THE FOLGER SHAKESPEARE LIBRARY.

Hollis, Thomas. Mr. G. V. Brooke as Othello (1839 to 1843).
ART FILE B872 NO.2A, IMAGE 21252. USED BY PERMISSION OF THE FOLGER SHAKESPEARE LIBRARY.

Sharkey, Bert. Walter Hampden as Othello (1900 to 1930).
ART FILE H229 NO.4, IMAGE 28567. USED BY PERMISSION OF THE FOLGER SHAKESPEARE LIBRARY.

Cowper, Max. "Set you down this . . . I took by the throat the circumcised dog and smote him thus" (1905).
ART BOX C876 NO.5, IMAGE 35822. USED BY PERMISSION OF THE FOLGER SHAKESPEARE LIBRARY.

If you are a teacher,
you are doing the world's most important work.
This book is for you.

CONTENTS

THE FOLGER GUIDE
TO TEACHING *OTHELLO*

PART ONE

Shakespeare for a Changing World

Why Shakespeare?

Michael Witmore

You have more in common with the person seated next to you on a bus, at a sporting event, or a concert than you will ever have with William Shakespeare. The England he grew up in nearly 400 years ago had some of the features of our world today, but modern developments such as industry, mass communication, global networks, and democracy did not exist. His country was ruled by a monarch, and his days were divided into hours by church bells rather than a watch or a phone. The religion practiced around him was chosen by the state, as were the colors he could wear when he went out in public.

When Shakespeare thought of our planet, there were no satellites to show him a green and blue ball. The Northern European island where he grew up was, by our standards, racially homogeneous, although we do know that there were Africans, Asians, Native Americans, Muslims, Jews, and others living in London in the early 1600s—and that Shakespeare likely saw or knew about them. The very idea that people of different backgrounds could live in a democracy would probably have struck him as absurd. What could an English playwright living centuries ago possibly say about our changed and changing world? Would he understand the conflicts that dominate our politics, the "isms" that shape reception of his work? What would he make of debates about freedom, the fairness of our economies, or the fragility of our planet?

The conversation about Shakespeare over the last 250 years has created other obstacles and distance. Starting around that time, artists and promoters put Shakespeare on a pedestal so high that he became almost divine. One such promoter was an English actor named David Garrick, who erected a classical temple to Shakespeare in 1756 and filled it with "relics" from Shakespeare's life. Garrick praised Shakespeare as "the God of our idolatry," and in his temple included a throne-like chair made of wood from a tree that Shakespeare may have planted. Today, that chair sits in a nook at the Folger Shakespeare Library. The chair's existence reminds us that the impulse to put Shakespeare in a temple has been at times overwhelming. But temples can exclude as well as elevate, which is why the Folger Shakespeare Library—itself a monument to Shakespeare built in 1932—needs to celebrate a writer whose audience is contemporary, diverse, and growing.

While Shakespeare was and is truly an amazing writer, the "worship" of his talent becomes problematic as soon as it is expected. If Shakespeare's stories and poetry continue to be enjoyed and passed along, it should be because we see their value, not because we have been told that they are great. Today, if someone tells you that Shakespeare's appeal is "universal," you might take away the idea that his works represent the experience of everyone, or that someone can only be fully human if they appreciate and enjoy his work. Can that possibly be true? How can one appreciate or enjoy the things in his work that are offensive and degrading—for example, the racism and sexism that come so easily to several of his characters? What about such plays as *The Merchant of Venice, Othello,* or *The Taming of the Shrew,* where the outcomes suggest that certain kinds of characters—a Jew, an African, a woman—deserve to suffer?

When we talk about Shakespeare, we have to confront these facts and appreciate the blind spots in his plays, blind spots that are still real and reach beyond his specific culture. In acknowledging such facts, we are actually in a better position to appreciate Shakespeare's incredible talent as a writer and creator of stories. Yes, he wrote from a dated perspective of a Northern European man who was a frequent flatterer of kings and queens. Within those limits, he is nevertheless able to dazzle with his poetry and offer insights into human motivations. We are not *required* to appreciate the language or dramatic arcs of his characters, but we can appreciate both with the help of talented teachers or moving performances. Memorable phrases such as Hamlet's "To be or not to be" are worth understanding because they capture a situation perfectly—the moment when someone asks, "Why go on?" By pausing on this question, we learn something at a distance, without having to suffer through everything that prompts Hamlet to say these famous words.

Had Shakespeare's plays not been published and reanimated in performance over the last few centuries, these stories would no longer be remembered. Yet the tales of Lady Macbeth or Richard III still populate the stories we tell today. They survive in the phrases that such characters use and the archetypal situations in which these characters appear—"out, out damned spot" or "my kingdom for a horse!" Marvel characters and professional politicians regularly channel Shakespeare. When a supervillain turns to the camera to brag about their evil deeds, we are hearing echoes of King Richard III. When the media criticizes a leader for being power-hungry, some version of Lady Macbeth is often implied, especially if that leader is a woman.

While they are from another time, Shakespeare's characters and situations remain exciting because they view life from a perspective that is both familiar and distant. The better able we are to recognize the experiences described in Shakespeare's plays in our lives, the broader our vocabulary becomes for understanding ourselves. We see and hear more when the plays dramatize important questions, such as:

- What does a child owe a parent and what does a parent owe their child? Why must children sometimes teach their parents to grow up? *King Lear, Hamlet,* and *Henry IV, Part 1* all ask some version of these questions.

- Are we born ready to love or is the capacity to love another something that is learned? Shakespeare's comedies—*Twelfth Night, As You Like It, Much Ado About Nothing*—are filled with characters whose entire stories are about learning to accept and give love.

- How does one deal with an awful memory or the knowledge of a brutal crime? Hamlet is burdened with both, just as many are today who are haunted by trauma.

These questions get at situations that anyone might experience at some point in their life. If you are a teenager whose mad crush is turning into love, you will have to go out on that balcony, just like Juliet. Will you be confident or afraid? If a "friend" who knows you well is feeding you lies, you will be challenged to resist them—as Othello is when faced with Iago. Will you be able to think for yourself? These questions come up in any life, and the answers are not predetermined. A goal in any humanities classroom is to improve the questions we ask ourselves by engaging our specific experiences, something very different from looking for "timeless truths" in the past.

Do not believe that you must master Shakespeare in order to appreciate literature, language, or the human condition. Do, however, be confident that the time you and your students spend with these plays will result in insight, new skills, and pleasure. Shakespeare was a deeply creative person in a deeply polarized world, one where religious and economic conflicts regularly led to violence. He used that creativity to illustrate the many ways human beings need to be saved from themselves, even if they sometimes resist what they need most. He also understood that stories can change minds even when the facts cannot. If there was ever a time to appreciate these insights, it is now.

The Folger Teaching Guides are the product of decades of experience and conversation with talented educators and students. The Folger continues to offer teachers the best and most effective techniques for cultivating students' abilities in the classroom, starting with Shakespeare but opening out on the great range of writers and experiences your students can explore. We invite you to visit the Folger in person in Washington, DC, where our exhibitions, performances, and programs put into practice the methods and insights you will find here. And we extend our gratitude to you for doing the most important work in the world, which deserves the dedicated support we are providing in these guides.

Good Books, Great Books, Monumental Texts—Shakespeare, Relevance, and New Audiences: GenZ and Beyond

Jocelyn A. Chadwick

"People can find small parts of themselves in each character and learn what it may be like to let the hidden parts of themselves out. Regardless of personal background, everyone can relate to the humanity and vulnerability that is revealed in Shakespeare's works." (Student 2023)

" 'To me, there is no such thing as black or yellow Shakespeare,' Mr. Earle Hyman, a celebrated African-American actor said. 'There is good Shakespeare or bad Shakespeare. It's simply a matter of good training and opportunity.' " ("Papp Starts a Shakespeare Repertory Troupe Made Up Entirely of Black and Hispanic Actors," *New York Times*, January 21, 1979)

"The question for us now is to be or not to be. Oh no, this Shakespearean question. For 13 days this question could have been asked but now I can give you a definitive answer. It's definitely yes, to be." (President Volodymyr Zelensky's speech to the UK Parliament, March 8, 2022)

"I, at least, do not intend to live without Aeschylus or William Shakespeare, or James, or Twain, or Hawthorne, or Melville, etc., etc., etc." (Toni Morrison, "Unspeakable Things Unspoken: The Afro-American Presence in Literature," *The Source of Self-Regard*, 2019)

How have William Shakespeare's brilliant and probing plays about the human condition come to an either/or to some contemporary audiences? The preceding quotes reveal appreciation, understanding, and metaphorical applications along with definitions of the playwright's depth and breadth. And yet, a misunderstanding *and* sometimes *conscious cancellation* of the man, his work, and his impact have undergone substantial *misunderstanding and misinterpretation*.

For as long as any of us can or will remember, William Shakespeare has continued to be with us and our students. True, this is a bold and assertive declarative statement; however, in the 21st century, is it and will it continue to be accurate and still *valid*?

Playwright Robert Greene, a contemporary of William Shakespeare, did not think much of Shakespeare's work or his talent:

> There is an upstart Crow, beautified with our feathers that with his Tygers hart wrapt in a Players hyde, supposes he is as well able to bombast out a blank verse as the best of you: and being an absolute Johannes factotum is in his owne conceit the onely Shake-scene in a country. (Robert Greene, *Greene's Groats-Worth of Wit*, 1592)

Clearly, Greene was jealous of Shakespeare's popularity and talent.

Interestingly, what Greene objects to parallels some 21st-century perspectives that at this writing recommend removal of Shakespeare's plays and poetry from curricula throughout the country—*just because.* For Greene, the objection was Shakespeare's talent, his appeal to his contemporary audience, his rising popularity, and cross-cultural exposure—not only angering Greene, but also resulting in his undeniable jealousy.

Today, however, the primary argument is that Shakespeare's texts are old and dated; he is white, and male—all of which from this perspective identify him, his time, and his work as disconnected from the realities of 21st-century students: antiquated, anachronistic, even racially tinged. These arguments persist, even though without doubt, Shakespeare's London was metropolitan, multicultural, and influenced by the city's international trade—imports as well as exports.

And further, to be clear, as Toni Morrison and so many other scholars, writers, *and* readers have asserted, the *durability* of a text lies with its present *and* future audiences. I should add here that Morrison was engaging with, and "talking back to," Shakespeare's play *Othello* when she wrote her play *Desdemona* in 2011.

At this writing, there are a number of contemporary catalysts pointing out the necessity of rethinking, reflection, and consubstantiation of such texts that have long been a part of the canon. We are experiencing not only that resurgence but also a book-banning tsunami in schools and public libraries. The result of such movements and actions indeed causes us to rethink; they have also compelled educators at all levels, parents, librarians, writers, and GenZ students to speak up and out.

To illustrate concretely students' responses, this essay necessarily includes the perspectives and voices from some high school students (grades 9–12), who attend Commonwealth Governors School (CGS) in Virginia. I asked a number of them what they thought about Shakespeare, and they told me. Their statements are in *their own words;* I did no editing. In addition, the students within the CGS system represent the panoply of inclusion and diversity.

> It's the big ideas that make Shakespeare relevant to myself and other students. Everyone loves, and everyone feels pain, so while we each might experience these feelings at different points in our lives, in different degrees, and for different reasons than others, I think Shakespeare's work is enough out of our times so that all students can connect to his themes and imagine themselves in the positions of his characters. (Student, May 2023)

And . . .

> I feel his general influence; I feel like he created a lot of literary words, and musicians like Taylor Swift draw from the works of earlier people, and Shakespeare continues to be relevant. (Student, 2023)

Interestingly, students *tapestry* what they read and experience in Shakespeare's works into their contemporary world, concomitantly, reflecting Umberto Eco's assertion about the import, impact, and protean qualities of a text's life: students create their own meaning and connections—building onto and extending Shakespeare's words, expression, characters, and challenges, ultimately scaffolding into their present realities, experiences, and challenges.

With all of these developments and conversations in mind, this Folger series of teaching guides provides that crossroad and intersection of analysis and rethinking. The central question that joins both those who see at present limited or no redeemable value in Shakespeare and those who view these texts as windows of the past, present, and, yes, the future is *"Do William Shakespeare's plays resonate, connect, and speak to 21st-century readers of all ages, and especially to our new generations of students?"*

Let us consider Eco's assertion: each time playwrights, directors, and artists reinterpret, every text undergoes a disruption, thereby reflecting new audiences. To *re-see* a character or setting when producing Shakespeare's plays is with each iteration a kind of disruption—a disruption designed to bring Shakespeare's 16th-century texts to audiences from multiple perspectives and epochs. The term *disruption* here takes on a more modern definition, a more protean and productive definition: Every time a reader enters a text—one of Shakespeare's plays, to be specific—that reader can meld, align, interweave experiences, memories, thoughts, aspirations, and fears, and yes, as the first student quote alludes, empower the reader to *identify* with characters, and moments and consequences. This reading and/or viewing is indeed a positive kind of disruption—*not to harm or destroy;* on the contrary, a positive disruption that expands and interrelates both reader and viewer with Shakespeare and each play. Past and present intersect for each generation of readers. In this positive disruption texts remain relevant, alive, and *speak verisimilitude.*

Similarly, we ask 21st-century students studying Shakespeare to bring their *whole selves* to the work, and to come up with their own interpretations. Allowing and privileging 21st-century students to compare and contrast and then examine, inquire, and express their own perspectives and voices remains the primary goal of English Language Arts: independent thinking, a developed voice, and the ability to think and discern critically for oneself. Both the primary text and adaptations are reflections *and* extended lenses:

The man i' th' moon's too slow—till new-born chins
Be rough and razorable; she that from whom
We all were sea-swallowed, though some cast again,
And by that destiny to perform an act
Whereof what's past is prologue, what to come
In your and my discharge (The Tempest 2.1, 285–89).

Just as the past continuously informs and reminds the present, the present—each new generation—brings new eyes, new thoughts, new perspectives. Of course, each generation sees itself as unique and completely different; however, the echoes of the past are and will always be ever-present.

In so many *unexpected* ways, the 21st-century Shakespeare audience in school—students, teachers, and others—share far more with William Shakespeare and his time than we may initially recognize and acknowledge. From his infancy to his death, Shakespeare and his world closely paralleled and reflects ours: upheavals and substantial shifts culturally, sociopolitically, scientifically, and religiously, as well as the always-evolving human condition. Each of the plays represented in this series—*Hamlet, Macbeth, Othello, Romeo and Juliet,* and *A Midsummer Night's Dream*—illustrates just how much William Shakespeare not only observed and lived with and among tragedy, comedy, cultural diversity, challenges, and new explorations, but also, from childhood, honed his perspective of both past and present and—as Toni Morrison expresses—*rememoried* it in his plays and poems. Tragedy and Comedy is rooted in the antiquities of Greek, Roman, and Greco-Roman literature and history. William Shakespeare uniquely crafts these genres to reflect and inform his own time; more importantly, the plays he left us foreshadow past and future connections for audiences to come—audiences who would encounter cross-cultures, ethnicities, genders, geography, even time itself.

More than at any other time in our collective history experienced through literature, the past's ability to inform, advise, and even "cushion" challenges our students' experiences today. It will continue to do so into the foreseeable future and will continue to support and inform, and yes, even protect them. Protecting, meaning that what we and our students can read and experience from the safe distance literature provides, allows, even encourages, readers to process, reflect, and think about how we respond, engage, inquire, and learn.

> The play . . . *Macbeth* . . . is about pride; there are lots of common human themes. He's the basis for a lot of literature like *Hamlet* is just the *Lion King;* it is just *Hamlet,* but it's lions. (Student, May 2023)

One fascinating trait of GenZ readers I find so important is the how of their processing and relating canonical texts to other contemporary texts and other genres around them: TV, movies, songs, even advertisements. What I so admire and respect about students' processing is their critical thinking and their ability to create new and different comprehension pathways that relate to their own here and now. In this new instructional paradigm, we *all* are exploring, discovering, and learning together, with William Shakespeare as our reading nucleus.

Although many writers and playwrights preceded William Shakespeare, his scope and depth far exceeded that of his predecessors and even his peers. His constant depiction and examinations of the human condition writ large and illustrated from a myriad of perspectives, times, cultures, and worlds set Shakespeare decidedly apart. The result of his depth and scope not only previewed the immediate future following his death, but more profoundly, his thematic threads, characters, settings, and cross-cultural inclusions continue to illustrate *us to us.*

The pivotal and critical point here is GenZ's continued reading and experiencing of William Shakespeare's plays. As they experience this playwright, they take bits and pieces of what they have read and experienced directly into other texts they read and experience in classes and daily living. In fact, in the "tidbits" they experience initially through Shakespeare, students will connect and interpret *and make their own meaning and connections,* even *outside* of textual reading. Malcolm X, in fact, provides us with an example of how that works:

> I read once, passingly, about a man named Shakespeare. I only read about him passingly, but I remember one thing he wrote that kind of moved me. He put it in the mouth of Hamlet, I think, it was, who said, "To be or not to be." He was in doubt about something—whether it was nobler in the mind of man to suffer the slings and arrows of outrageous fortune—moderation—or to take up arms against a sea of troubles and by opposing end them. And I go for that. If you take up arms, you'll end it, but if you sit around and wait for the one who's in power to make up his mind that he should end it, you'll be waiting a long time. And in my opinion the young generation of whites, blacks, browns, whatever else there is, you're living at a time of extremism, a time of revolution, and now there has to be a change and a better world has to be built, and the only way it's going to be built—is with extreme methods. And I, for one, will join with anyone—I don't care what color you are—as long as you want to change this miserable condition that exists on this earth. (Oxford Union Queen and Country Debate, Oxford University, December 3, 1964)

Like Malcolm X, GenZ students turn toward the wind, staring directly and earnestly into their present and future, determined to exert their voices and perspectives. Their exposure to past and present literature, sciences, histories, and humanities allows, even empowers, this unique generation to say, "I choose my destiny." And the myriad texts to which we expose them informs, challenges, and compels them to always push back and move toward a truth and empowerment *they* seek. Some of us who are older may very well find such empowerment disconcerting—not of the "old ways." But then, just what is a comprehensive education for lifelong literacy supposed to do, if not expose, awaken, engage, even challenge and open new, prescient doors of inquiry, exploration, and discovery? This is the broad scope of not just education for education's sake but of reading and experiencing for oneself *devoid of outside agendas—whatever they may be or from wherever they may emanate.*

A student put this succinctly:

> Elements of his writing are still relevant in today's films and books, like his strong emotional themes, tropes, and character archetypes. Shakespeare's works are quoted often by common people [everyday people] and even by more influential individuals, including civil rights leader Martin Luther King, Jr., who was known to quote Shakespeare often. I believe the beautiful and unique work by William Shakespeare is still greatly relevant and appreciated now and will go on to remain relevant for centuries more. (Student, May 2023)

The plays comprising this series represent curricula inclusion around the country and also represent the angst some parents, activists, and politicians, even some fearful teachers, have about our continuing to include Shakespeare's works. That said, there are many, many teachers who continue to teach William Shakespeare's plays, not only allowing students from all walks of life to experience the man, his time, and the sheer scope of his thematic and powerful reach, but also privileging the voices and perspectives GenZ brings to the texts:

> We can see in Shakespeare our contemporary and sometimes frightening range of humanity today—I am specifically thinking of our current political turmoil—is not unique, and that just like the evil monarchs such as Richard III appear in Shakespeare's plays, they are always counterbalanced by bright rays of hope: in *Romeo and Juliet,* the union between the Montagues and Capulets at play's end restoring peace and civility . . . It is impossible for me to watch any performance or read any Shakespeare play—especially the tragedies—without leaving the theatre buoyed up by hope and respect for humankind, a deeper appreciation of the uses of the English language, and a feeling that I have been on a cathartic journey that leaves my students and me enriched, strengthened, and hopeful. (Winona Siegmund, Teacher, CGS)

> I'm going to be honest, I'm not very knowledgeable on the subject of Shakespeare . . . I never really went out of my way to understand and retain it. All I know is that I can't escape him. No matter how hard I try, and trust me, I try, he will always be somewhere, running through the media with his "art thous" and biting of thumbs. Perhaps people see themselves in the plays of Shakespeare. Maybe Shakespeare is a dramatization of the hardships we experience every day . . . Shakespeare has stained my life. One of those annoying stains that you can't get out. A bright, colorful stain that's easy to notice. But who cares? It was an ugly shirt anyway; might as well add some color. (Student, May 2023)

> Taylor Swift's "Love Story." I LOVE the STORY of *Romeo and Juliet.* See what I did there? But in all honesty, there are so many Shakespeare-inspired works (*Rotten Tomatoes*, *West Side Story*, *Twelfth Grade Night*, etc.) that I liked and remained relevant to me, and prove that Shakespeare will always be relevant. The first Shakespeare play I read was *Macbeth* when I was twelve and going to school in Azerbaijan. And even as a preteen studying in a foreign country, I loved the story and found it morbid, funny, and wise all at the same time. My Azerbaijani classmates liked it, too. Due to this unique experience, I think that anyone can enjoy and identify with Shakespeare's works, no matter their age or country of origin. (Student, May 2023)

The five plays in this Folger series represent the universal and social depth and breadth of all Shakespeare's poetry and plays—verisimilitude, relevance, *our* human condition—all writ large in the 21st century and beyond. Through characters, locations, time periods, challenges, and *difference,* William Shakespeare takes us all into real-life moments and decisions and actions—even into our *not yet known or experienced*—to illustrate the human thread joining and holding us all as one.

> Despite being several hundred years old, Shakespeare's works have yet to become antiquated. There are several reasons for this long-lasting relevance—namely the enduring themes. Shakespeare's themes on humanity, morality, loss, and love remain relatable for people across all walks of life. (Student, May 2023)

In sum, a colleague asked me quite recently, "Jocelyn, why do you think students just don't want to read?" To add to this query, at this writing, I have tracked an increasing, and to be honest, disturbing sentiment expressed on social media: some teachers positing, essentially, the same perspective. My response to both is the same: our students—elementary through graduate school—*do* read and write every day. They will also read what we assign in our classes. However, this generation of students first thinks or asks outright—*Why?* What do I *get* if I invest the time and effort? Most assuredly direct inquiries with which many veteran teachers *and* professors are unfamiliar—perhaps even resentful. But let's be honest. Our students of a now-patinated past most likely felt the same way. Remember the plethora of *CliffsNotes* and *Monarch Notes*? I know I threw my share of students' copies in the trash—wanting them to read for themselves.

Just like adults, our students, especially today, have a right to ask us *Why*? What *do* they *get* if they invest their time in reading assigned texts? Umberto Eco brilliantly answers why our students *must* continue reading and experiencing texts—for this series, William Shakespeare's plays—and learning through performance:

> Now a text, once it is written, no longer has anyone behind it; it has, on the contrary, when it survives, and for as long as it survives, thousands of interpreters ahead of it. Their reading of it generates other texts, which can be paraphrase, commentary, carefree exploitation, translation into other signs, words, images, even into music. ("Waiting for the Millennium," *FMR No. 2,* July 1981, 66)

To illustrate Eco's assertion, I will leave it to one student and two people with whom all teachers and many students are familiar:

> Shakespeare's work is relevant because his legacy allows people from all walks of life to understand that they can make a difference. Although people from all walks of life may not always relate to his works, the impact that he made on modern literature and theater is undeniable. The lasting dreams that his works have provided for young people lay the groundwork for our future. Shakespeare's living works are proof that one small man with one small pen can change the future of everything around him. (Student, May 2023)

I met and fell in love with Shakespeare . . . It was a state with which I felt myself most familiar. I pacified myself about his whiteness by saying after all he had been dead so long it couldn't matter to anyone anymore. (Maya Angelou on her childhood introduction to and love of Shakespeare in *I Know Why the Caged Bird Sings*, 1969)

and, as Malcolm X proclaimed:

I go for that. (Oxford Union Queen and Country Debate, Oxford University, December 3, 1964)

Why This Book?

Peggy O'Brien

First, let's start with YOU: If you are a schoolteacher, know that you are the most precious resource in the world. In every school, town, city, state, country, civilization, universe, or solar system, there is none more valuable than you. It is hard, hard work, and yet . . . you are doing the most important work on earth. Period.

At the Folger Shakespeare Library, we know this well and deeply, and that's why you are a clear focus of our work. If you teach Shakespeare and other complex literature—and particularly if you are a middle or high school teacher—it is our mission, passion, and honor to serve you. Therefore . . . welcome to *The Folger Guides to Teaching Shakespeare* and our five volumes on teaching *Hamlet, Macbeth, Othello, Romeo and Juliet,* and *A Midsummer Night's Dream*.

Here's why this book: our overall purpose. We know that many of you find yourselves teaching plays that you don't know well, or that you've taught so often that they are beginning to bore you to death. (You talk to us, and we listen.) So, these books give you fresh information and hopefully meaningful new ideas about the plays you teach most frequently, along with a very specific way to teach them to all students—high-fliers, slow readers, the gamut. We see the Shakespeare content and the teaching methodology as one whole.

We often get these questions from y'all. You may recognize some or all of these:

- How on earth do I even begin to think about teaching a Shakespeare play? No one has really ever taught me how to teach Shakespeare and my own experience with Shakespeare as a high school student was . . . not great.

- How can Shakespeare possibly make sense in this day and age? In this changing world? Old dead white guy?

- Shakespeare can't possibly be engaging to all my students, right? I mean, it's true that really only the brightest kids will "get" Shakespeare, right?

- SO . . . what's the Folger Method and how does it fit into all of this?

- I have to teach the "10th-grade Shakespeare play"—whatever it is—and I haven't read it since high school, or maybe I have never read it.

- I'm a schoolteacher and don't have extra time to spend studying up before I teach this stuff.

15

- Doesn't using those watered-down, "modernized" Shakespeare texts make it easier? Aren't they the most obvious way to go?

- Can learning and teaching Shakespeare really be a great experience for my kids and for me too?

Our *Folger Guides to Teaching Shakespeare* is hopefully an answer to these questions too.

Here's why this book: the Folger Method. At the Folger, not only are we home to the largest Shakespeare collection in the world but we have developed, over the last four decades or so, a way of teaching Shakespeare and other complex texts that is effective for *all* students. We're talking well-developed content and methodology from the same source, and in your case, *in the same book.* Imagine!

The Folger Method is language-based, student-centered, interactive, and rigorous, and it provides all students with ways into the language and therefore into the plays. Our focus is words, because the words are where Shakespeare started, and where scholars, actors, directors, and editors start. Shakespeare's language turns out to be not a barrier but *the way in.* The lessons in this book are sequenced carefully, scaffolding your students' path. They will find themselves close-reading, figuring out and understanding language, characters, and the questions that the play is asking. All of this when they may have started out with "Why doesn't he write in English?" It's pretty delicious. If you want to know more about the Folger Method right this minute, go to the chapter that starts on page 43.

A few things I want you to know right off the bat:

- Because the Folger Method involves lots of classroom work that is interactive and exciting (and even joyful), sometimes teachers are tempted to pull a few lessons out of this book and use them to spruce up whatever they usually do. Oh resist, please. Take the whole path and see what your students learn and what you learn.

- There is no "right" interpretation of any play (or work of literature for that matter). In working with the Folger Method principles and essentials, your students come up with their own sense of what's going on in *Othello.* Their own interpretation. Not yours, or the interpretation of famous literary critics, but their own. And then they bring it to life. Exciting! That's what we're after because the skills that they'll develop in doing this—close-reading, analysis, collaboration, research—they will use forever.

- The Folger Method may call on you to teach differently than you have before. Be brave! You are not the explainer or the translator or the connector between your students and Shakespeare. You're the architect who sets up the ways in which Shakespeare and your students discover each other . . . and we'll show you very explicitly how to do that.

Here's why this book: parts of the whole. Each of these guides is organized in the same way:

- **Part One is the big picture:** Folger director Michael Witmore and Jocelyn Chadwick both take on the "Why Shakespeare?" question from very different angles. And Jocelyn brings students into the conversation too. Delicious!

- **Part Two is YOU and *Othello*.** Through a set of short takes and one delicious long take, you'll get a stronger sense of the play. The shorts are some speedy and pretty painless ways to learn both the basics and a few surprises about both *Othello* and Shakespeare.

  The long take is "Liberating *Othello* from Shakespeare's Bondage: Race and Identity," an essay written for you by Ambereen Dadabhoy and Kim F. Hall, two accomplished and celebrated Shakespeare scholars. Kim, in fact, was one of the first scholars who began to look at Shakespeare through the lens of race—and still leads that work today. We know that you have no "extra" time ever, but we also know that schoolteachers find connecting with new scholarship to be enlivening and compelling. New ways to look at old plays—new ways most often sparked by the changing world in which we live—continue to open up many new ways to look at Shakespeare. What you take away from Ambereen and Kim's essay may show up in your teaching soon, or maybe at some point, or maybe never—and all of those are good. You may agree with or grasp their perspective on *Othello,* or you may not; they will get you thinking, though—as they get us thinking all the time—and that's what we're about.

- **Part Three is you, *Othello*, your students, and what happens in your classroom.**

  - The Folger Method is laid out clearly—and bonus: with the kind of energy that it produces in classrooms—so that you can get a sense of the foundational principles and practices before you all get into those lessons, and your own classroom starts buzzing.

  - A five-week *Othello* unit, day-by-day lessons for your classes, with accompanying resources and/or handouts for each. We know that the people who are the smartest and most talented and creative about the "how" of teaching are those who are working in middle and high school classrooms every day. So, working schoolteachers created all of the "What Happens in Your Classroom" section of this book. They do what you do every day. While these writers were writing, testing, and revising for you and your classroom, they were teaching their own middle and high school kids in their own. And I am not mentioning their family obligations or even whispering the word "pandemic." At the Folger, we are in awe of them, and for many of the same reasons, are in awe of all of you.

  - Two essays full of practical advice about two groups of students whom teachers ask us about often. The first details and demonstrates the affinity that English Learners and Shakespeare and *Othello* have for one another. The second focuses on the deep connections that can flourish between students with intellectual and emotional disabilities and Shakespeare and *Othello*. No barriers to Shakespeare anywhere here.

  - The last essay is packed with information and examples on pairing texts—how we make sure that students are exposed to the broad sweep of literature while at the same time are busy taking Shakespeare right off that pedestal and into conversations with authors of other centuries, races, genders, ethnicities, and cultures. This is where magic starts to happen!

And now . . . back to YOU! Get busy! Othello says "Here is my journey's end . . . ," but this is your beginning! An energized and meaningful journey of mutual discovery is at hand—both for you and your students. Tell us how it all goes. As always, we want to know *everything*!

PART TWO

Getting Up to Speed, or Reviving Your Spirit, with *Othello*

Ten Amazing Things You May Not Know About Shakespeare

Catherine Loomis and Michael LoMonico

The basics: Shakespeare was a playwright, poet, and actor who grew up in the market town of Stratford-upon-Avon, England, spent his professional life in London, and returned to Stratford a wealthy landowner. He was born in 1564—the same year that Galileo was born and Michelangelo died. Shakespeare died in 1616, and Cervantes did too.

1. In the summer of 1564, an outbreak of bubonic plague killed one out of every seven people in Stratford, but the newborn William Shakespeare survived.

2. In Shakespeare's family, the women were made of sterner stuff: Shakespeare's mother, his sister Joan, his wife Anne Hathaway, their daughters, and granddaughter all outlived their husbands. And Joan lived longer than all four of her Shakespeare brothers. The sad exception is Shakespeare's younger sister Anne. She died when she was seven and Shakespeare was fifteen.

3. Shakespeare appears in public records up until 1585, when he was a 21-year-old father of three, and then not until 1592, when he turns up in London as a playwright. During those lost years, he may have been a schoolmaster or tutor, and one legend has him fleeing to London to escape prosecution for deer poaching. No one has any idea really, but maybe there is a theatrical possibility: an acting company called the Queen's Men was on tour in the summer of 1587, and, since one of their actors had been killed in a duel in Oxford, the town just up the road, the company arrived in Stratford minus one actor. At age 23, did Shakespeare leave his family and join them on tour?

4. Shakespeare wrote globally: in addition to all over Britain, his plays take you to Italy, Greece, Egypt, Turkey, Spain, France, Austria, Cyprus, Denmark and, in the case of *The Tempest*, pretty close to what was to become America.

5. Shakespeare died of a killer hangover. The Reverend John Ward, a Stratford vicar, wrote about Shakespeare's death on April 23, 1616, this way: "Shakespeare, [Michael] Drayton, and Ben Jonson had a merry meeting, and it seems drank too hard, for Shakespeare died of a fever there contracted."

6. On Shakespeare's gravestone in Stratford's Holy Trinity Church is a fierce curse on anyone who "Moves My Bones." In 2016, archeologists used ground-penetrating sonar to examine the grave, and . . . Shakespeare's skull is missing.

7. Frederick Douglass escaped slavery and as a free man became a celebrated orator, statesman, and leader of the American abolitionist movement—and he was a student and lover of Shakespeare. Visitors to Cedar Hill, his home in DC's Anacostia neighborhood, can see Douglass's volumes of Shakespeare's complete works still on his library shelves and a framed print of Othello and Desdemona on the parlor wall. In addition to studying and often referencing Shakespeare in his speeches, Douglass was an active member of his local Anacostia community theater group, the Uniontown Shakespeare Club.

8. Shakespeare is the most frequently produced playwright in the U.S. Despite this, *American Theatre* magazine has never crowned him America's "Most Produced Playwright," an honor bestowed annually based on data from nearly 400 theaters. He always wins by such a big margin—usually there are about five times more Shakespeare productions than plays by the second-place finisher—that the magazine decided to just set him aside so that other playwrights could have a chance to win.

9. While Nelson Mandela was incarcerated on South Africa's Robben Island, one of the other political prisoners retained a copy of Shakespeare's complete works, and secretly circulated it through the group. At his request, many of the other prisoners—including Mandela—signed their names next to their favorite passages.

> *Cowards die many times before their deaths;*
> *The valiant only taste of death but once.*
> *Of all the wonders that I yet have heard,*
> *It seems to me most strange that men should fear,*
> *Seeing that death, a necessary end,*
> *Will come when it will come.*

These lines from *Julius Caesar* were marked and signed "N. R. Mandela, December 16, 1977." Nelson Mandela was released from prison in 1990.

10. The Folger Shakespeare Library is in Washington, DC, and houses the largest Shakespeare collection in the world, just a block from the U.S. Capitol. We are Shakespeare's home in America! We are abuzz with visitors and audience members from our own DC neighborhoods, from across the country and around the world: teachers and students, researchers and scholars, lovers of the performing arts, all kinds of learners, and the curious of all ages and stages. Find us online at teaching.folger.edu—and do come visit our beautiful new spaces. Be a part of our lively and accessible exhibitions and programs, explore rare books and other artifacts, join a teaching workshop, and enjoy the magic of theatre, poetry, and music. We're waiting for you, your classes, and your families!

Ten Amazing Things You May Not Know About *Othello*

Patricia Akhimie, Catherine Loomis, and Michael LoMonico

1. As he did with almost every play, Shakespeare took ideas for the plot of *Othello* from an existing story—a short novel with no title, written in 1565 by Cinthio, an Italian writer and professor also known as Giovanni Battista Giraldi. The characters who we would identify as Othello and Iago are unnamed and only called the Moor and the Ensign.

2. *Othello* was first performed at court, for James I in 1604. It was performed outdoors at the Globe Theatre and in Oxford in 1610, and even later, multiple times at Shakespeare's indoor Blackfriars Theatre. In celebration of the wedding of James's daughter Princess Elizabeth, *Othello* was performed again at court in 1612.

3. The first appearance of a professional actress on the English stage was in a production of *Othello* in December 1660. Margaret Hughes played Desdemona.

4. Iago is the third-largest part in all of Shakespeare's plays—the character has 1,097 lines; only Hamlet and Richard III have more. By comparison, Othello has only 860 lines. Words appearing frequently in *Othello* are "love" (used 80 times), "heaven" (60), "Moor" (45), "honest" (42), "time" (29), "handkerchief" (28), and "fair" meaning "white" (22).

5. Scholars who study Shakespeare's use of language across all of the plays have discovered that conversations between Othello and Iago are full of the same kind of seductive, courtship-like language found in Shakespeare's comedies. Who is seducing whom? And why?

6. Othello is called a "Moor," a term with many different meanings in Shakespeare's time: it was used to identify someone of North African origin, or Muslim faith, or Berber or Arab ethnicity, or simply someone with darker skin, or some or all of these. In the play, who refers to Othello as "Moor" rather than by name, and when and why do they do so?

7. The role of Othello was first played by Richard Burbage, a white actor in Shakespeare's acting company. Burbage and the hundreds of other white actors who played the part over the centuries since then used various techniques to darken their skin, such as makeup made of soot and grease. Othello continued to be played by white men in blackface from the first performance of the play in 1604 until 1833 when, in London, American actor Ira Aldridge became the first Black man to play Othello in a professional production.

8. In 1852, during the United States' Gold Rush, Edwin Booth—generally acknowledged as the finest American Shakespearean actor of his time—played Iago in a production of *Othello* performed at a mining camp in Grass Valley, Nevada. A popular story claimed that Booth was so convincing as the villain that when Othello fails to kill Iago in the play's final scene, members of the audience drew their guns and began shooting at Iago/Booth. This story about Booth may be the basis of a popular tale about another production of *Othello* in the 19th-century American West: during the last scene of the play, the actor playing Othello was shot and killed by an audience member who was trying to prevent him from killing Desdemona.

9. Ira Aldridge's portrayal of Othello was a one-time occurrence: only white men in blackface played Othello for the next hundred years—until 1930. Paul Robeson, a Black American actor, concert singer, lawyer, activist, and football all-American, played Othello with a white Desdemona in a 1930 London production. In 1943, he played Othello in the U.S. on Broadway, the first Black actor to play Othello in a major American production. After seeing his performance on Broadway, W. E. B. Du Bois, in an editorial, wondered if a white actor would ever play the role again. The production ran on Broadway for 296 performances before going on a national tour to both northern and southern cities. Robeson's contract made clear that he would not play in any theaters in which the audiences were racially segregated.

10. The Folger Shakespeare Library offers visitors, scholars, teachers, and theatergoers lots of ways to experience *Othello*. The Folger collection houses 382 stand-alone printed editions of *Othello* in roughly 36 different languages: Albanian, Arabic, Armenian, Bengali, Bulgarian, Chinese, Croatian, Czech, Dutch or Flemish, English, Esperanto, French, Georgian, German, Greek (Modern), Hebrew, Icelandic, Italian, Kannada, Karachay-Balkar, Lithuanian, Norwegian, Persian, Polish, Portuguese, Romanian (Moldavian and Moldovan), Russian, Serbian, Slovenian, Spanish (and Castilian), Swedish, Tegulu, Thai, Turkish (and Ottoman 1500–1928), Urdu, and Yiddish.

The Folger Theatre has produced *Othello* four times, including a 1990 production in which the roles of Othello and Iago were both played by Black actors. At the Folger Institute, the research hub of the Folger, research fellows and participants in scholarly programs work to understand the historical context of *Othello* and contribute new critical commentary. As part of Folger Education's work, we work with teachers on ways to teach *Othello*—and ways to engage students in conversations about race—through online professional development, the Teaching Shakespeare Institute, Summer Academies, and courses such as *Teaching Shakespeare IS Teaching Race*.

What Happens in This Play Anyway?

A Plot Summary of *Othello*

In Venice, at the start of *Othello,* the soldier Iago announces his hatred for his commander, Othello, a Moor. Othello has promoted Cassio, not Iago, to be his lieutenant.

Iago crudely informs Brabantio, Desdemona's father, that Othello and Desdemona have eloped. Before the Venetian Senate, Brabantio accuses Othello of bewitching Desdemona. The Senators wish to send Othello to Cyprus, which is under threat from Turkey. They bring Desdemona before them. She tells of her love for Othello, and the marriage stands. The Senate agrees to let her join Othello in Cyprus.

In Cyprus, Iago continues to plot against Othello and Cassio. He lures Cassio into a drunken fight, for which Cassio loses his new rank; Cassio, at Iago's urging, then begs Desdemona to intervene. Iago uses this and other ploys—misinterpreted conversations, insinuations, and a lost handkerchief—to convince Othello that Desdemona and Cassio are lovers. Othello goes mad with jealousy and later smothers Desdemona on their marriage bed, only to learn of Iago's treachery. He then kills himself.

What Happens in This Play Anyway?

A PLAY MAP OF *OTHELLO*

Mya Gosling and Peggy O'Brien

There's a lot going on in *OTHELLO!*

Othello, a decorated general, has just secretly married **Desdemona**, the daughter of **Brabantio**, a senator.

Othello is Black. Desdemona is white. Brabantio does not approve.

Iago expects to be promoted as Othello's lieutenant, but Othello promotes Michael Cassio instead.

Iago is jealous. Very jealous.

What does Iago do with his jealousy? How does Othello and Desdemona's marriage get on?

Who has the power and when? Who manipulates whom?

What happens in a play...that has lines like this?

"Valiant Othello!"

"Your son-in-law is far more fair than black."

"It is their husbands' faults if wives do fall."

"Let her rot and perish and be damned tonight."

"I will poison his delight."

"I have not deserved this."

"Reputation, reputation... I have lost my reputation!"

"She was chaste. She loved thee."

Who's Who?

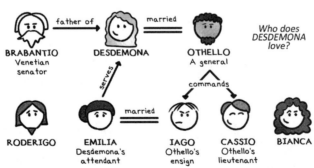

BRABANTIO — Venetian senator — *father of* → **DESDEMONA** — *married* → **OTHELLO** A general

Who does DESDEMONA love?

RODERIGO

EMILIA Desdemona's attendant — *married* — **IAGO** Othello's ensign — *commands* — **CASSIO** Othello's lieutenant

BIANCA

Who on earth is RODERIGO, and what's his role?

Why is EMILIA really important?

Who does IAGO hate, and why?

Who is BIANCA and what's her story?

Art by Mya Lixian Gosling of goodticklebrain.com. Concept by Peggy O'Brien.

"She gave me for my pains a world of [kisses.]"

"I follow him to serve my turn upon him."

"Come, come, you're drunk."

"My lord, you know I love you!"

"Look to your wife. Observe her well."

"I shall against the Moor."

"My heart has turned to stone."

"One that loved not wisely but too well."

Liberating Othello from Shakespeare's Bondage: Race and Identity

Ambereen Dadabhoy and Kim F. Hall

In his introduction to the Oxford edition of *Othello*, Michael Neill points out that *Othello* has become *the* Shakespearean play that speaks to the multicultural society of the twenty-first century. Neill suggests that the play addresses the world we live in because of the problem at its center: Othello's insider/outsider status and the limits of his assimilation into Venetian culture and society. The diversity that the play seems to offer through its non-European and non-white character and its dialogue about inclusion may also be why so many choose to teach this play.

To read *Othello* through the lens of multiculturalism requires questioning how cultural, religious, and racial differences are accepted and embraced by the dominant culture in society. It demands looking into the ways that characters like Othello can belong and not belong within their adopted culture. It also requires analysis of how the culture's own biases and prejudices might hinder or limit belonging, making people's acceptance conditional and tenuous. *Othello*'s plot relies upon these kinds of cultural boundaries, and Othello's character can be understood through his own violations and enforcement of those cultural boundaries and limitations. Readers should, however, be aware of the dangerous forked message of *Othello:* that tolerance is not acceptance and that racism deeply disturbs and disrupts the tidy narratives of diversity and multiculturalism that we might be tempted to read into this play.

In the twentieth century—and perhaps coincidentally with Othello becoming a role exclusively for Black actors—it seemed that readers and critics wanted to turn away from Othello's blackness. One way this manifested was by promoting the myth that emerged in the nineteenth century that Othello was a "tawny" Moor of brown complexion rather than a white actor in carefully applied black makeup. This Arabized Othello seemed to fit in with the play's geopolitics as well as sideline its black-white racial politics. These interpretations also abstracted the play into transcendent questions of love and jealousy rather than delving into its striking concerns with interracial marriage, whiteness, and racial belonging. The play both promises and denies insights into Black identity, a conversation that has, until recently, been dominated by white scholars and theater makers. However, the twenty-first century has seen an increase in "respeakings" of *Othello* by Black writers, actors, and artists: their works offer new possibilities for thinking about *Othello* beyond diversity, and as part of a larger conversation about race/blackness/social difference in theater, and in thinking about Shakespeare's works beyond attributing the character to an articulation of Shakespeare's genius. These conversations ask: What does it mean to see Othello's blackness?

Othello and "the terrible bed of history"

Making the play speak for multicultural societies like that in the United States and the United Kingdom can often mean that the play's target audience is white, and that white people are given the illusion that *Othello* explains the experience of minorities within these societies. However, Nigerian-British poet Ben Okri points out the problematic stakes for audiences and readers in seeing Shakespeare's representation of Black identity:

> It doesn't really matter that Shakespeare didn't, and quite possibly couldn't, get Othello fully in focus nor looked at him closely enough. What matters is that because of Shakespeare's genius Othello haunts the English stage. He won't go away. He is always there on the stage, a reminder of his unexplained presence in the white consciousness, and as a symbol of the fact that black people and white are bound on the terrible bed of history. Doomed to his relentless cycle, he will not vanish from our dreams. And yet I dream of ways of liberating him from that bondage. (87)

Okri's analysis of Shakespeare's shortcomings with Othello, the play's enduring racial resonances within societies structured by white dominance, and the emotional pull that Othello exerts for Black and white people captures the many complexities of engaging with this play. While Othello cannot be "liberated from the bondage" of Shakespeare's script—meaning that he cannot be freed from the plot that has trapped him as a duped wife-murderer—readerly and scholarly responses attuned to and informed by the operations of racism and anti-blackness can uncover how they inform and structure his character and his journey. These investigations can also encourage students to explore how Black artists have intervened in Othello's narrative, offering a perspective that Shakespeare could not have imagined. In this way we can challenge ways of reading that can be oblivious to how race is a culturally ingrained, learned way of reading that supports racial hierarchy. Avoiding race is an abdication of our responsibility as teachers to prepare students for life beyond the classroom. Scholar Ian Smith reminds us that together we can learn racial literacy to avoid the racial obliviousness that is a tool of "systemic whiteness" (3). We can also take Othello's final exhortation, "Speak of me as I am" (5.2.401), as a call to learn the workings of racism that ensnare both Othello and Desdemona.

To pick up *Othello* now and to study it means wrestling with the difficulties contained in its representation of race and how that representation travels across time to affect Black people and their lives. It provides a potent and enduring example for everyone on the powers of representation and language in creating hierarchies of humanity and enacting exclusion. To read *Othello* is to think simultaneously about the past and the present: it is to address timely and urgent concerns about racial injustice and systemic racism, not because Shakespeare has the answers for us, but because Shakespeare unintentionally offers us warnings about assimilation, minority identity, sexism, and "systemic whiteness." Tackling the topic of race and racism head-on better equips students, teachers, actors, and others to understand Othello's uneasy position within the world Shakespeare has created for him. Approaching the play with the racial tensions it animates at the forefront of our thinking can make visible the intersection of the social and racial hierarchies of the play and reveal how these hierarchies marginalize, dehumanize, and alienate those people who are marked as Other because of their non-whiteness.

To understand how race works in *Othello,* it is important to understand what race is. By "race" we mean the social and cultural manufacturing of human difference, often along lines of embodied difference such as skin color, to create dominant and subordinate groups. While people do have different skin colors, hair textures, and bodily features, the meanings ascribed to the body by a culture interested in creating hierarchical access to social and tangible resources based on those qualities are what transform physical difference into race. These differences take on a social meaning and are artificially created, but they have material effects, regardless of whether groups or individuals are seen to possess race (non-whites) or to be racially unmarked (whites). Behaviors based on race, especially ones that capitalize on the accrual of advantages and punishment of disadvantages, are forms of racism. Race and racism operate within and through other systems of domination and subordination such as sex and class. Therefore, race and racism are often in dialogue with other "interlocking systems of oppression," as Black feminist scholar bell hooks notes, and so, as Black feminists have taught, must always be analyzed along other categories.

Othello's racial difference may be one reason that Othello isn't "fully in focus," as Okri suggests. This lack of clarity about the character is demonstrated by the play's very structure, which conspires against its hero in a way unusual for Shakespeare's eponymous tragedies: the dramatic and linguistic turns of the play point to its discomfort with its hero's own blackness. The play opens with the markings of comedy—a couple who marry against a father's wishes; a concern with cuckoldry and jealousy; determinedly urban settings; a world of braggarts, dupes, and fools. The suspicion of the marriage, set up from the play's opening, turns into ongoing surveillance of the couple and is cast in racial/racist terms. Much of this suspicion and spying is set up by Iago, who has more lines than the "tragic hero" and dramatically competes with Othello for our attention, which he seems to control by the end of the first act. Iago's framing of Othello will be contradicted by Othello's appearance onstage as a somber and sober military commander, yet the meanings attached to Iago's racist and color-coded images in the initial construction of Othello will haunt him for the remainder of the action. His own reservedness as a character, "My parts, my title, and my perfect soul / shall manifest me rightly" (1.2.36–37), harms him as stereotypes and preconceptions swirl around the stage and with readers and audiences. We hear of a tantalizing backstory—what does it mean for a middle-aged man of war to find love for the first time? What violence marks his past? There is a certain unknowability to his character: the intimacy one might expect from friends, and even his wife, rapidly evaporates. He has no confidantes—no Hamlet's Horatio, no Desdemona's Emilia—only an enemy he does not know about who pretends to be his closest ally. Characters become estranged from him fairly soon after their arrival in Cyprus. Moments of vulnerability that should allow the audience to connect with him, like his seizure, may only serve to emphasize his singularity and strangeness.

Moors

In its subtitle, "the Moor of Venice," and throughout the play, Othello is referred to by the epithet "Moor." This term, while seeming to explain Othello's ethnicity or race, is rather more symbolically loaded than initially appears. "Moor" is a designation that is both broad and imprecise, suggesting people of African origin, Islamic faith, and/ or Black skin. In the England of Shakespeare's time, the term's inexactness allowed it to be applied indiscriminately to several non-white and non-Christian peoples. We can only be sure that "Moor" designates someone who is not a European Christian. In *Othello*, the geography over which "Moor" holds significance includes Africa and the Ottoman Empire. While there were ethnic differences between Moors and Ottomans (called "Turks" in European writing) in the period, their shared religion, Islam, often brought them into mistaken alignment for early modern Europeans. Unlike several of his contemporaries whose plays about Moors were set in the western Mediterranean, such as George Peele's *The Battle of Alcazar* (1594), Shakespeare moves the action of his play farther east, into a Mediterranean dominated by the Ottoman Empire and its advances into Venetian territories such as Cyprus. Within this geography of imperial competition and aggression, the epithet "Moor" links Othello to "the general enemy, Ottoman," but with a difference demonstrated both by his race and his religious affiliation (1.3.57). The identity marker "Moor" allows Othello to occupy an "other" space, where he is separated from both Venice and the Ottoman Empire and linked to Africa through his blackness. "Moor" signals Othello's racial difference from all other characters in the play and the threat posed by the Ottomans at its borders. Consequently, the term highlights the tolerance of white Venetian society that has become his new home, which embraces Othello as a successful military commander against their enemies, but it emphasizes the limits of that tolerance, because as a Moor he is ineligible to be a bridegroom for an elite Venetian woman.

Race as Spectacle and Sensation

Othello is animated by the spectacle of black and white. Far from blackness and race being supplemental to the play, *Othello* immerses us in language, makeup, costumes, and props that indicate racialized meanings in material, symbolic, and sensory ways. Audiences of the London stages as well as its playwrights would have been eager consumers of the influx of written materials about Others that was driven by a renewed growth in global travel and trade. This fascination went from page to stage: early modern audiences across Europe anticipated theatrical innovation and came to expect Black characters and performers to exhibit particular forms of "Black" appearance, speech, and movement (Ndiaye). On the London stage, blackness was being transformed into a stage trope, a generally understood way of being, a stereotype.

From its opening, the play is dark, loud, and cacophonous. The riotous rousing of Brabantio from his sleep is paralleled by the thundering tempest routing the "general enemy Ottoman," signaling the play's heightened sonic registers (1.3.57). The play's soundscape heightens the tensions of the plot and reinforces the sense that Othello's presence and its effect on the community, such as through his elopement with Desdemona, constitute a state of emergency. While recounting to the Senate how he wooed and won Desdemona's love, Othello unfolds the story of his life, travels, adventures, and sorrows, noting that this was a tale that Brabantio, too, often wanted to hear: "Her father loved me, oft invited me, / Still questioned me the story of my life" (1.3.149–150). Through this narrative, Othello reveals Desdemona's eager participation in their courtship:

> *These things to hear*
> *Would Desdemona seriously incline.*
> *But still the house affairs would draw her thence,*
> *Which ever as she could with haste dispatch,*
> *She'd come again and with a greedy ear*
> *Devour up my discourse.*
>
> *. . . .*
>
> *My story being done,*
> *She gave me for my pains a world of sighs.*
> *She swore, in faith, 'twas strange, 'twas passing strange,*
> *'Twas pitiful, 'twas wondrous pitiful.*
> *She wished she had not heard it, yet she wished*
> *That heaven had made her such a man. . . . (1.3.168–188)*

Othello's description points to Desdemona's own yearning. She "inclines" toward his stories, hungrily consuming them with her "greedy," acquisitive, and perhaps insatiable ear. Indeed, her desire to hear again, in full, his "pilgrimage," emphasizes her gluttonous appetite for his stories, his voice, and his presence. In Othello's retelling, Desdemona is an active agent, as much a wooer as she is wooed. Even as he recounts Desdemona's eager desire, Othello's speech reveals the same desire in his Venetian audience; they, too, are rapt in their attention and feed on his story. Black feminist critic bell hooks calls such moments of white consumption of non-white life, being, and personhood "eating the Other," a formulation through which whiteness vicariously experiences some of the "spice" and exoticism of non-whiteness (21). In this scene, Othello's speech neatly aligns with the elevated and accepted norms of elite (white) rhetoric; however, in performance, modes of acting then and now can signal various forms of blackness. The monologue itself and the vocal patterns and intonations of the Black actor's performance rely on the vocal and sonic allure of Othello's difference, on the sound of the Black actor's voice speaking these words. The play corroborates this attraction when the Duke proclaims, "I think this tale would win my daughter, too" (1.3.197). The persuasive power of Othello's voice and speech gesture toward the dangers of intimacy with the non-white racialized Other. It highlights how contact with difference can lead to desire rather than fear.

In addition to paying attention to the ways the play focuses on Othello's language, it is useful to think about the many stage practices that helped create a sense of Othello's shocking difference onstage. In both early modern and later blackface performances, Othello's blackness has a spectacular appeal, meaning that it is a sight to behold. Black makeup, along with black cloth or leather, was used to reproduce the sense of a living

Black body onstage. Conversely, the boy actor playing Desdemona would have worn highly stylized white makeup, emphasizing her femininity and desirability, while also literally hiding the male face underneath. These deliberate fabrications of race as both blackness and whiteness expose the many tangible resources put to work to make race serve the social and political needs of the dominant group.

The handkerchief is perhaps the most important stage prop in all of Shakespeare's plays because of the many meanings and histories that come to be attached to it. Othello gifts the handkerchief to Desdemona as a symbol of his love, but once she loses it, the handkerchief is swiftly transformed into the external sign of her chastity and fidelity. In addition to carrying the weight of the romance, the handkerchief is another tangible reminder of the play's racial and gender politics. Because the plot depends so heavily on the handkerchief, it has drawn much critical attention, from derisive commentary that the play is the tragedy of a misplaced napkin to feminist interventions exposing the link between the handkerchief and the spotted bedsheets that signal a consummated marriage. These interpretations link the handkerchief to Desdemona's sexuality and chastity. It is a symbol of her faithfulness yet can be easily transformed into a sign of her faithlessness. Moreover, the handkerchief is also implicated in the racial discourse that animates the play: when its purity, as a symbol of their marriage, is put into question by its loss and its circulation through many hands, then so, too, is Desdemona soiled by that same circulation. Desdemona's fairness is tied to her sexual purity, as Othello indicates when he says "was this fair paper, this most goodly book, / Made to write 'whore' upon?" (4.2.82–83). Having succumbed to Iago's persuasions about Desdemona's infidelity and having seen the handkerchief in Cassio's possession, Othello's accusation of infidelity utilizes racial metaphors. Desdemona's white skin, "the fair paper," has been blotted by the word "whore." In Othello's view, her whiteness is corrupted through her impure sexual desires. Shakespeare's depiction of interracial marriage in this play calls into question Desdemona's racial purity. Her real and perceived sexual desire places her outside the acceptable norms and boundaries of whiteness.

The handkerchief's origin story makes it a vehicle for non-white racialization as well. The story highlights the object's cultural roots and demonstrates Othello's racial isolation within his adopted culture. Part of Othello's cultural inheritance from his mother, the handkerchief is steeped in the wondrous exotica he earlier evoked before the Senate:

That handkerchief
Did an Egyptian to my mother give.
She was a charmer, and could almost read
The thoughts of people. She told her, while she kept it
'Twould make her amiable and subdue my father
Entirely to her love. But if she lost it
Or made a gift of it, my father's eye
Should hold her loathèd, and his spirits should haunt
After new fancies. She, dying, gave it me,
And bid me, when my fate would have me wived,
To give it her. I did so; and take heed on 't;
Make it a darling like your precious eye.
To lose 't or give 't away, were such perdition
As nothing else could match. (3.4.65–79)

Othello's narrative makes the handkerchief a talisman that secures, protects, and nurtures love, so long as it is kept safe; however, its loss foreshadows the destruction of that same love, and so love fulfilled becomes love lost. Embedded in this history is a warning to Desdemona that she treat the handkerchief as irreplaceable because it represents Othello, his body as well as his love (Smith, 14–15). If it is lost, then he is lost to her. Othello's recounting further attributes the handkerchief's history to his mother and, before her, to the Egyptian "charmer" who gave it to her. Indeed, Othello tells Desdemona that the handkerchief's magical capacities are rooted in its very fabric:

> *There's magic in the web of it.*
> *A sibyl that had numbers in the world*
> *The sun to course two hundred compasses,*
> *In her prophetic fury sewed the work;*
> *The worms were hallowed that did breed the silk,*
> *And it was dyed in mummy, which the skillful*
> *Conserved of maidens' hearts. (3.4.81–87)*

Taken as a whole, Othello's story racializes the handkerchief through the very same associations of sorcery and witchcraft that Brabantio accuses him of at the beginning of the play. In reclaiming such properties for the handkerchief, Othello confirms those associations with his Africanness and his blackness. The handkerchief's genealogy emphasizes this "magic" in its own geographic and supernatural positioning through references to the "Egyptian charmer" and the "mummy" used to dye the cloth. Moreover, the feminine origin and transmission of the handkerchief signals the absent presence of Othello's own family and community. While African women do not appear in the play, they are recalled through the handkerchief and its racialized erotic powers. Their conjuring in this manner allows Othello an interpretive frame through which to understand his wife's apparent disloyalty and betrayal. In this account, the handkerchief, its story, and the meanings that have been culturally assigned to it allow Othello some level of surety in an arena where knowledge is actively being withheld from him by Iago. Its manipulation in the play (it literally passes through many hands—Othello's, Desdemona's, Emilia's, Iago's, Cassio's, and Bianca's) and the eroticism with which it is imbued demonstrate its tactile significance: it becomes a substitute for Othello and Desdemona for all those who seek intimacy with them.

Fair Ladies, Whiteness, and Expectations for Marriage

Othello's symbol of whiteness is the young, headstrong Desdemona, who contracts an illicit marriage with a man outside of her social, cultural, and racial milieu. If Othello is "the Moor of Venice," with all of the contradictions and ambiguities that term implies, Desdemona's identity is bound up in her elite status as Brabantio's daughter. However, her marriage to Othello imperils her status and her whiteness, which rests on her social and cultural belonging as well as her chastity, modesty, and virtue. The play situates the forbidden romance between Othello and Desdemona along the color line, coded through the antagonism it locates in Brabantio's patriarchal authority and the conventions of Venetian society.

For Renaissance elites, *fairness* was not just a marker of beauty and status, it was a way to mark race; that is to say, it identified those worthy of admiration, desire, social, and (almost literal) credit. Offering access to political, social, and economic power, it was a quality so valuable that it demanded celebration and reproduction. Through its opposition to blackness, whiteness manifests in the play's first scene, with Iago's obscene recital of interracial sex, and continues through its final moments, which feature the corrupted nuptial bed loaded with the grisly sight of the intertwined bodies of Desdemona and Othello. Desdemona is portrayed as having a social responsibility to reproduce that fairness with a proper marriage. Iago heightens Othello's sense of Desdemona as untrustworthy by noting that her disobedience began by turning down men more suited to her status: "As, to be bold with you, / Not to affect many proposèd matches / Of her own clime, complexion, and degree" (3.3.268–70). He then closes by naturalizing racial categorization: "Whereto we see in all things nature tends" (3.3.271). Similarly, for Brabantio, Desdemona must be protected from a man like Othello, whose blackness signals his aggression and desire for her and in the face of which she should quake in terror. Tellingly, the Duke attempts to resolve the problem of the conundrum of the mixed marriage by metaphorically "whitening" Othello: "Your son-in-law is far more fair than black" (1.3.331).

The language of fair beauty is one of the ways that racial distinctions are made to appear "natural" and normal. Because it operates on so many different levels, the politics of fairness can be difficult to pin down. However, fairness and whiteness have particular implications for early modern women. Fairness becomes a way for men to differentiate between women. One can see in many other plays characters proclaiming their beloved fairer than other women. In *A Midsummer Night's Dream*, for example, Helena bemoans the fact that she is not accounted as fair as Hermia, who is desired by Demetrius, the man that Helena loves. Later in the play, however, when she is the object of desire for both Lysander and Demetrius, they attempt to win her favor by proclaiming her fairness in contrast with Hermia's newly constructed foreign darkness (1.1; 3.2). Frequently, this is not an innocent assessment of an individual woman's beauty, but a way of creating competition between women for patriarchal approval and, most important, of disciplining women's behavior.

Like whiteness, fairness was meant to be a rare and exclusive property. For women, it could be easily marred and lost. This instability of whiteness was most frequently exercised/marked on the bodies of women and can be seen clearly in accusations of cosmetic whitening or painting, despite the fact that cosmetics were an important part of early modern life for both men and women (Karim-Cooper). *Othello* hit the stage at the end of the reign of a queen, Elizabeth I, who used the association of whiteness with purity, chastity, and femininity to mark her political power as the Virgin Queen. Her whiteness became more pronounced in her own cosmetic practice and in her portraiture during her reign.

However, because it was meant to be valuable and exclusive, whiteness for ordinary women was dangerously unstable. In the Senate scene, where she must confess her love for Othello and her own agency in the romance plot and elopement, Desdemona is aware that she is defaming herself, and in a way, staining the purity of her whiteness with her erotic desires: "That I love the Moor to live with him / My downright violence and scorn of fortunes / May trumpet to the world" (1.3.283–285). In addition to losing their whiteness through the exercise of desire, women were accused of achieving whiteness through the "fraud" of cosmetics rather than virtue and natural beauty. When Othello is at the height of his suspicion, he sees Desdemona's tears as a form of deceit, "O, well-painted passion!" (4.1.291). In playing out paradoxes of fairness/blackness, the somewhat obscure back-and-forth joking between Desdemona and Iago at the beginning of Act 2 reinforces the slander that women are subjected to and the insecure place of the fair woman.

Indeed, the move to Cyprus exposes the fragility of Desdemona's social position, which was only foreshadowed in Venice. Iago's success in hinting at a covert relationship between Cassio and Desdemona depends on Othello's racial difference, on Cassio's and Desdemona's racial and class similarity, and on Iago's own racial insider status. In response to Othello's claim that "she had eyes, and chose me," Iago notes, "In Venice they do let God see the pranks / They dare not show their husbands" (3.3.220; 233–234). Positioning himself as an authority on Venetian women and, therefore, an authority on Desdemona's character and sexual purity (or lack thereof), Iago capitalizes on Othello's social and cultural ignorance in addition to his blackness. As Othello continues to ruminate on the possibility of his wife's faithlessness, he begins to find its cause in their racial difference: "And yet how nature, erring from itself" (3.3.267). As noted above, Iago seizes on Othello's insecurity to further emphasize the racial divide: "Ay, there's the point. As, to be bold with you, / Not to affect many proposèd matches / Of her own clime, complexion, and degree, / Whereto we see in all things nature tends—" (3.3.268–271). Desdemona's whiteness, here, is upheld by both Othello and Iago as a behavioral inclination that should prevent her from desiring Othello. Seeming convinced of his wife's betrayal, Othello again attributes the cause to his race: "Haply for I am black / And have not those soft parts of conversation / That chamberers have" (3.3.304–306). He denies in himself precisely those qualities that Cassio possesses, combined with the physical characteristics Iago calls forth. Cassio is thus framed as Othello's opposite both in character and in race. In pointing out his own blackness, Othello simultaneously notes the whiteness of the other characters and the mutual, racialized bonds of community and desire they all share and from which he is barred.

As we have sketched above, the play's use of fairness as a racialized value links Desdemona's racial purity through her sexual innocence. Iago's plot to destroy Othello hinges on cultural notions of women's inherent disloyalty and unruly sexual appetites, as well as on patriarchal anxiety about emasculation. Confronted by Othello's accusations of sexual impropriety, Desdemona proclaims her chastity through the language of Christian purity. In response to Othello's challenge, "Are not you a strumpet?," she defends herself by professing "No, as I am a Christian! / If to preserve the vessel for my lord / From any other foul unlawful touch / Be not to be a strumpet, I am none" (4.2.94–98). Othello's rebuke of her character is rooted in color-coded language meant to mar and tarnish her character, "Was this fair paper, this most goodly book / Made to write 'whore' upon?," and all of Desdemona's rebuttals pick up those allusions to insist on her innocence through the racialized language of Christianity (4.2.82–83). As a Christian woman she is pure, saved, not sullied or "foul," and therefore white and innocent of the sexual crimes of which Othello accuses her. Indeed, her plan to "lay on my bed my wedding sheets" is another symbolic reminder of her sexual purity (4.2.122). The wedding sheets presumably testify to her virginity, with bloody evidence of its loss to her husband. These white sheets verify her sexual innocence (whiteness) and refute the accusations leveled at her by her husband, yet, conversely, they are not sufficient evidence because patriarchal logic dictates that a woman's innocence can only be claimed once; after that, she can offer no tangible evidence toward her sexual purity. The only clear sign of her chastity, then, is "that whiter skin of hers than snow, / And smooth as monumental alabaster" (5.2.4–5). For Othello, her whiteness belies the corruption of her character, but as the racial logic of the play makes apparent, this whiteness should in and of itself be a transparent sign of her virtue. Othello's inability to read her correctly is attributed to patriarchal paranoia and racial difference. The play insistently links her whiteness with innocence in order to transform her into a symbol of martyred white womanhood. Othello's murder of her is a patriarchal honor killing. Desdemona is murdered because she has violated Othello's honor through her sexual infidelity. To reclaim his honor and manhood Othello must destroy her. Additionally, the murder forever demonizes Othello because it is depicted as an act of Black rage.

Respeaking *Othello*

Othello is a powerful play. Over the centuries, both the eponymous character and Shakespeare have acquired the right to speak for and about Black lives. Challenging the presumed multiculturalism of the play, however, readers, audiences, and, especially students are resisting uncritical acceptance of the play's racial underpinnings. Students have begun to "talk back to Shakespeare." They are joined by artists, scholars, and writers of color who dispute the privilege afforded to Shakespeare and his play. Their works engage with its damaging and problematic race logic and representations in ways that call attention to the limits of the Shakespearean imagination. From Djanet Sears to Toni Morrison to Phoebe Boswell to Keith Hamilton Cobb, Black artists, writers, and intellectuals have responded to Shakespeare's work by stretching the Shakespearean text with their interventions to make it speak for and through them.

We have here chosen to preview a few revisions of *Othello* that interrogate race and blackness in important ways, which not every adaptation or appropriation does. Our focus on the Anglo-American tradition means that our selection here is by no means exhaustive: there are several revisions from the vast array of identity groups belonging to the African diaspora as well as from African and other cultures of the Global South, such as Tayeb Salih's *Season of Migration to the North* (1966) and Vishal Bhardwaj's film *Omkara* (2006), that offer important disruptions to and expansions of Shakespeare. The Afro-diasporic interventions we highlight provide new directions for Othello that destabilize Shakespeare's centrality in the construction of Black identity.

Engagement with such revisions and respeakings of *Othello* is necessary when we teach the play because Othello cannot remain an authority on Black life or on race. Both Djanet Sears's *Harlem Duet* and Toni Morrison's *Desdemona,* for example, consent to and challenge Shakespeare's narrative by shifting their artistic focus to the marginalized Black and African women who haunt but are not physically on-stage in *Othello.* By prioritizing the lives, histories, concerns, and emotions of Black and African women, Sears and Morrison not only expose critical absences in the play but also lay bare the white lies at the heart of Shakespeare's depictions. Sears's *Harlem Duet* explores and expands the story of *Othello* in three different timelines in Harlem, the 1860s, 1920, and the present. Through two main characters, Her and Him, She and He, and Othello and Billie, Sears weaves a layered examination of Black love, Black pain, and Black women's complex experiences under the twin power hierarchies of racism and misogyny. Although the characters move across historical eras, setting the play in their Harlem apartment insists on a certain intimacy that reinforces the play's thesis that the personal is political: seemingly personal erotic desires are implicated in larger networks of race and power. Billie/Sybil highlights the erasure of Black women in Shakespeare's work as well as the marginalization of Black women within Anglo-American culture. Sears affirms Billie's power through memory and family, through history and genealogy, allowing for a resolution in which Billie finds the home that was lost through all of the incarnations of her story.

Similarly, Toni Morrison's *Desdemona* gives voice to Shakespeare's forgotten African women, most significantly by reimagining Barbary, whose "willow song" Desdemona sings as she prepares for her eventual doom, in the form of Sa'ran, an enslaved woman in Brabantio's household. Where Desdemona seeks love from and identification with "Barbary," Sa'ran points out the impossibility of such a relation because of her enslaved status, which denies her humanity, dignity, and agency. Morrison's play, written in collaboration with Malian musician Rokia Traoré, takes place in the afterlife where time "has no meaning," and so offers limitless possibility for apology, restitution, and forgiveness (55). While Desdemona is the main character whose life and journey are the filters through which the play materializes, African women, such as Othello's mother and Sa'ran, are given body and voice through both Morrison's words and Traoré's songs so that their lives and experiences can be perceived and therefore legitimized, acts of mutual recognition not offered by Shakespeare's play.

Phoebe Boswell's short film *Dear Mr. Shakespeare* also emphasizes the critical absence of Black women in *Othello*. Boswell's film, a verse dialogue created to commemorate the four-hundredth anniversary of Shakespeare's death, questions Shakespeare's culpability as both playwright and cultural icon in the centuries of anti-Black racism that *Othello* seems to inaugurate and endorse. In under six minutes, the visceral images and poetry of Boswell's film respond to Shakespeare through his own theatrical traditions, while exploring and exploding the possibilities of engagement with *Othello*. (You may be teaching *Othello* well into the twenty-first century. At this writing, it is accessible at https://www.phoebeboswell.com/dear-mr-shakespeare/2017/3/13/dear-mr-shakespeare, and hopefully this accessibility will continue.) By positioning a Black woman as Shakespeare's equal and indeed, a forceful interlocutor, Boswell, like her predecessors, decenters Shakespeare's primacy on matters of race and even his authority over his own character, Othello.

Keith Hamilton Cobb's *American Moor* stages a conversation between a Black actor auditioning for the role of Othello and a white director who seems to know "what Shakespeare is trying to say here" (16). Cobb's play questions the racial hierarchies at work in both Venice and Cyprus even as it critiques how those systems manifest in American theater and its white-dominated theatrical productions. Through an exploration of the institution of the theater, how it is controlled by and conforms to white cultural, social, and monetary interests, Cobb interrogates other forms of gatekeeping within the Shakespeare industry designed to marginalize and circumscribe the possibilities of performances and roles available to Black actors. These exclusionary maneuvers, the play makes clear, are the same forces that restrict Black life outside of the theater industry as well. The play is also Cobb's sustained meditation on the possibilities of Black interiority in *Othello* (and other plays) if the controlling hand of whiteness can cede some creative power to the experience, knowledge, and skill of the Black actor. Ultimately, *American Moor* invites its audience to reimagine Shakespeare's play and the artistic process that allows it to come to life as a collaboration that acknowledges the humanity of the Black actor at the center of *Othello* and the urgent need for his powerful voice to be heard if we are to have potent dialogues about race and racism.

In the opening of this essay we note how for some, *Othello* has become the Shakespeare play that perfectly captures the human condition in the twenty-first century through its depictions of the cultural struggles of minority identities within white-dominant societies. Other critics, however, take a different view: Ayanna Thompson has quite persuasively argued that *Othello* is one of Shakespeare's toxic plays and so it should no longer be staged. Her argument relies on the problematic message of the play, wherein Othello will always be too gullible to recognize the trap that has been so successfully laid for him; thus, he is forever made the symbol of Black men's alleged desire for white women and their supposed propensity for violence. We respectfully disagree with this view and advocate for approaches to the play that are attentive to its insidious racialization and anti-blackness. It is necessary, then, for all of us—teachers, students, and audiences—to consider what "service" we may be doing via our engagement with the play. Are we expecting the play's multicultural meaning to come through without much effort on our parts? Or are we examining the racism at the play's center through deliberate anti-racist measures that call attention to the rigged social system that Othello inhabits? If we are unwilling to consign *Othello* to the dustbin of history, then we must do the latter. Along with its beautiful language and the marginalized position of its titular character, our teaching practices must be attuned to the play's damaging and dehumanizing messages as well. Even though our students are centuries removed from Shakespeare's writing of this play, they recognize in its racial dynamics their own world and how inclusion and exclusion continue to operate through the color line. *Othello* can only offer us answers if we include in our classroom practices the interventions of people of color who challenge and dissent from Shakespeare's representation and make the play speak in many languages and many traditions. These interventions underscore *Othello*'s power as a cultural touchstone even as they reveal why it is important that we do not allow Shakespeare to have the last word on *Othello*.

Bibliography and Suggested Reading

Adams, B. K. "Fair/Foul," in *Shakespeare / Text: Contemporary Readings in Textual Studies, Editing and Performance,* edited by Claire M. L. Bourne. London: Bloomsbury Arden Shakespeare (2021), 1–49.

Boose, Lynda E. "Othello's Handkerchief: 'The Recognizance and Pledge of Love.'" *English Literary Renaissance* 5.3 (1975): 360–374.

Britton, Dennis A. *Becoming Christian: Race, Reformation, and Early Modern English Romance.* New York: Fordham University Press (2014).

Cobb, Keith Hamilton. *American Moor.* London: Bloomsbury Publishing (2020).

Dadabhoy, Ambereen. "Two Faced: The Problem of Othello's Visage," in *Othello: The State of Play.* London: Bloomsbury (2014), 121–48.

Daileader, Celia R. "Casting black actors: beyond Othellophilia." *Shakespeare and Race* (2000): 177–202.

Erickson, Peter. " 'Late has no meaning here': Imagining a Second Chance in Toni Morrison's *Desdemona." Borrowers and Lenders: The Journal of Shakespeare and Appropriation* 8.1 (2013).

Hall, Kim F. *Things of Darkness: Economies of Race and Gender in Early Modern England.* Ithaca, NY: Cornell University Press (1995).

hooks, bell. "Eating the Other: Desire and Resistance," in *Black Looks: Race and Representation.* Boston, MA: South End Press (1992).

Karim-Cooper, Farah. *Cosmetics in Shakespearean and Renaissance Drama.* Edinburgh University Press (2006).

MacDonald, Joyce Green. *Shakespearean Adaptation, Race and Memory in the New World.* Palgrave Macmillan (2020), 109–134.

Mehdizadeh, Nedda. "Othello in Harlem: Transforming Theater in Djanet Sears's Harlem Duet." *Journal of American Studies* 54, no. 1 (February 2020): 12–18.

Morrison, Toni. *Desdemona.* London: Oberon Books (2012).

Ndiaye, Noémie. "Shakespeare, Race, and Globalization: *Titus Andronicus,*" in *The Cambridge Companion to Shakespeare and Race,* edited by Ayanna Thompson. Cambridge University Press (2020), 158–174.

Okri, Ben. "Leaping out of Shakespeare's terror: Five meditations on *Othello,*" in *A Way of Being Free* (1988), 71–87.

Royster, Francesca T. "Rememorializing *Othello:* Teaching *Othello* and the Cultural Memory of Racism," in *Approaches to Teaching Shakespeare's* Othello, edited by Peter Erickson and Maurice Hunt. New York: Modern Language Association (2005), 53–61.

Rymer, Thomas. *A Short View of Tragedy.* London, 1693.

Shakespeare, William. *Othello, the Moor of Venice,* edited by Michael Neill. *The Oxford Shakespeare.* Oxford: Oxford University Press (2006).

Smith, Ian. *Black Shakespeare: Reading and Misreading Race.* Cambridge: Cambridge University Press (2022).

—. "Othello's Black Handkerchief." *Shakespeare Quarterly* 64.1 (2013): 1–25.

Thompson, Ayanna. "Practicing a Theory/Theorizing a Practice: An Introduction to Shakespearean Colorblind Casting," in *Colorblind Shakespeare: New Perspectives on Race and Performance.* London: Routledge (2006), 1–24.

PART THREE

Othello in *Your* Classroom with *Your* Students

The Folger Method:
You Will Never Teach Literature
the Same Way Again

Corinne Viglietta and Peggy O'Brien

Imagine a classroom where every student is so immersed in reading that they don't want to stop. A place that is buzzing with the energy of student-driven learning. Where students shout, whisper, and play with lines from Shakespeare and other authors. Where small groups discuss, with textual evidence and passion, which parts of a text are the most compelling and how to perform them effectively. Where all students bring their identities and customs, their whole selves, to fresh performances of juicy scenes. Where every student experiences firsthand that literary language is *their* language, demanding to be interpreted and reinterpreted, questioned, and yes, even resisted sometimes. Where students are doing the lion's share of the work, and the teacher, who has thoughtfully set up this zone of discovery, is observing from the side. Where joy and rigor work hand in hand. Where everyone is engaged in something that feels important and adventurous. Where every student realizes they can do hard things on their own.

This is a real place. This is *your* classroom as you try the lessons in this book. Yes, *you*.

Will it be perfect all the time? Heck no. Will it be messy, especially at first? Almost certainly. Will you have to take risks? Yes.

Does this way of teaching really work? You bet.

Don't take our word for it, though. For four decades, the Folger has been working with teachers on what has become known as the Folger Method, and here's a small sample of what teachers—mostly middle and high school teachers—have had to say:

- *"With the Folger Method, my students are reading more deeply than they ever have before. They are breaking down language and really understanding it."*

- *"I was unsure of myself and my ability to tackle Shakespeare, but this has been empowering."*

- *"Students complain when it's time to leave. I have gleefully stepped back so they can create scenes, shout words and lines, and cut speeches. They volunteer to read aloud even when reading aloud is hard for them. We dive in and focus on the words. It's working."*

- *"Over the course of this Folger unit, I've seen amazing things in my special education students. This one student has had an entire transformation—like, fellow teachers are asking me what happened. Before, he always had great pronunciation and sounded fluent, but he could never really understand what it was he was saying. And then all of a sudden in the middle of this play, something clicked. I think it's because he has all these strategies for understanding the words on the page now."*

- *"The Folger Method didn't just transform how I teach Shakespeare—it's changed how I teach everything."*

Great, but what *is* the Folger Method, exactly?

It is a transformative way of approaching complex texts. (And not just Shakespeare, but any complex text.) Consisting of both principles and practices, it provides a framework for everything that goes into great teaching: designing, planning, assessing, reflecting, revising, communicating, guiding, growing, listening, laughing, learning—all of it.

Behind it all is a precise, tried-and-true philosophy that we've broken down into 8 parts.

8 Foundational Principles

The more you practice this way of teaching, the more you'll see these **8 foundational principles** in action, and the clearer it all becomes. Watching your students move through the lessons in this book will give you (and them) a profound, almost visceral, understanding of these principles. They will become part of the fabric of your classroom. Teaching this way—even if it's completely new to you—will feel intuitive in no time.

1. Shakespeare's language is not a barrier but a portal. The language is what enables students to discover amazing things in the texts, the world, and themselves.

2. All students and teachers deserve the real thing—whether it's Shakespeare's original language, primary source materials, new information that expands our understanding of history, or honest conversations about tough issues that the plays present.

3. Give up Shakespeare worship. If your Shakespeare lives on a pedestal, take him down and move him to a space where he can talk to everyday people and to great writers like Toni Morrison and Julia Alvarez, Frederick Douglass and Joy Harjo, F. Scott Fitzgerald and Azar Nafisi, Amy Tan and George Moses Horton, Jane Austen and Pablo Neruda, James Baldwin and Homer.

4. Throw out themes, tidy explanations, and the idea of a single right interpretation. Resist the urge to wrap up a text with a neat bow, or, as Billy Collins puts it, to tie it to a chair and "torture a confession out of it." With ambiguity comes possibility. Alongside your students, embrace the questions. How liberating!

5. The teacher is not the explainer but rather the architect. Set up the interactions through which your students and Shakespeare discover each other. This might be hard to hear (it was for Corinne at first!), but the helpful teacher is not the one who explains what the text means or who "translates" Shakespeare's words for students. The truly helpful teacher is the one who crafts opportunities for students to be successful at figuring things out for themselves. It's about getting out of the way so students can do things on their own.

6. Set students on fire with excitement about literature. When reading brings mysteries, delights, and surprises, students are motivated to read closely and cite evidence. And they gain confidence in their ability to tackle the next challenge.

7. Amplify the voice of every single student. Shakespeare has something to say to everybody, and everybody has something to say back to Shakespeare. Student voices, both literal and figurative, create the most vibrant and inclusive learning communities. The future of the humanities—and our world—depends on the insights and contributions of *all* students.

As tempting as it may be to impose our own interpretation of the text on students, or to ask students to imitate the brilliant arguments of seasoned scholars, we beg you to resist that urge. Students need to dive into a play and shape and reshape their own interpretations in order to become independent thinkers. Teaching literature is about the sparks that fly when readers of an infinite variety of perspectives engage directly and personally with the text.

8. The Folger Method is a radical engine for equity. Every student can learn this way, and every teacher can teach this way. The goal is to help all students read closely, interrogate actively, and make meaning from texts.

Now let's put these ideas into practice.

The Arc of Learning

The first step to applying these principles in class is understanding the journey, what we call the arc of learning, that your students will experience.

The activities in this book are not isolated, interchangeable exercises. They are a complete set of practices that work together to bring the 8 principles to life. Sequencing, scaffolding, pacing, differentiating—it's all here.

And because each of your students is unique, each journey will be unique too. If you teach AP or IB classes, this book will help each of your students navigate their own path and reach rigorous course outcomes, starting right where scholars, editors, directors, and actors start—with the words. If you teach students who have the ability and desire to dive deep—and we mean *deep*, luxuriating in the mysteries and puzzles of complex literature—the Folger Method will enable them to do just that. Alongside these students you probably also have students who need some extra support before diving deep, and these lessons are just as much for them (more on differentiation later). By its very design, this way of teaching is flexible and roomy enough to challenge and support every single learner. Use this book to meet *all* students where they are, give them space to stretch, and be amazed at what they do.

What happens over the course of a Folger unit often astonishes teachers, administrators, families, and students themselves. Remember that spirited classroom from the first paragraph? Pass by and hear students shouting lines from Desdemona or Othello in a cacophony. *(What in the world?)* Poke your head in and watch them mark up their scripts with notes on which words ought to be stressed or cut out entirely, which tone to use when. *(Hmmm . . . this is interesting.)* Walk into the classroom, take a seat, and observe different student performances of the same scene—and a robust whole-class discussion about the textual evidence and knowledge that led to each group's interpretive decisions. Listen to students question and teach one another. *(Whoa! Every single student just totally owned Shakespeare.)*

What at the start might appear simply as a "fun" way to meet Shakespeare's words reveals itself to be a wild and daring, deep and demanding, meaty and memorable learning experience. Behind this magic is a very deliberate design.

From day one, your students will engage directly with the language of the text(s). That's right: There's no "I do, we do, you do" teacher modeling here. Students are always doing, doing, doing. Beginning with single words and lines, your students will learn to read closely and critically and eventually tackle longer pieces of text such as speeches, scenes, text sets, and whole texts. (Real talk: Yes, scaffolding learning by increasing the length and complexity of the language means doing some prep work. It's part of being the architect. Good news: This book has already selected and chunked most of the text for you!) Like other teachers using this method, you will likely notice that pre-reading *is* reading, just in small bites. You'll also notice your students using and reusing strategies. Sometimes you'll revisit a strategy from Week One later in the unit, with a new piece of text or an added layer of complexity. For example, Choral Reading and Cutting a Scene are favorite classroom routines that teachers use multiple times not just in a Shakespeare unit but throughout the school year. Over time, as you progress through the lessons, you will observe your students doing literacy tasks that are increasingly demanding and sophisticated, and you'll all have gained a method to help you tackle any complex text.

The process of speaking lines, interrogating and editing text, negotiating meaning, deciding how language should be embodied and performed, and owning literature—and doing it all without much teacher explanation—is what matters most. Simply put, the process is more important than the product. Don't fret if the final product is not perfect (what human endeavor is "perfect," anyway?). Did the students collaborate to analyze language and create something new? Do they know what they're saying? Have they made Shakespeare's language their own? So what if a group's performance has some awkward pauses or someone mispronounces a word? If your students have been reading actively, asking and answering good questions, and reaching their own evidence-based conclusions, it's all good. The real work happens along the arc, not at the end.

9 Essential Practices

This is the moment in our live workshops when teachers typically tell us how simultaneously *excited* and *nervous* they are about trying the Folger Method.

Excited because the Principles, the Arc, the whole philosophy of turning the learning over to the students, speaks to their own deeply held conviction that all students can do much more than is often asked of them. As one high school English teacher put it, "These Principles express something I know deep down and want to act on."

Nervous because this Folger thing is really different from how most of us were taught in school. Exactly how does a teacher "act on" the 8 Foundational Principles? What happens in class? What does the teacher do and not do? What does the student do and learn? What do teachers and students have to "unlearn" or let go of in order to try this approach?

The answers to these questions lie in the nine core practices of the Folger Method—the 9 Essentials. Within the lessons that follow this chapter, you will find step-by-step instructions for these Essentials right when you need them. For now, we will provide you with a brief overview of each one.

1. Tone and Stress boosts students' confidence in speaking text aloud and explores how a text's meanings are revealed through vocal expression. Students experience firsthand how variations in tone of voice and word stress influence a listener's understanding of subtext. They see and hear that there's no single right way to interpret a text. Longtime teacher and Teaching Shakespeare Institute faculty member Mike Lo-Monico spent a lot of time and expertise developing this!

2. Tossing Words and Lines puts text into students' hands and mouths and gets them up on their feet reading, speaking, and analyzing the language together. Bonus: Students are able to make inferences about the text based on the words they encounter.

3. Two-line Scenes get all students up on their feet, creating and performing two-person mini-scenes. They discover how making collaborative decisions to enact text is exciting and reveals new understandings. They also realize they can encounter a text "cold" and make meaning from it all on their own—dispelling the myth that Shakespeare's language is too dense to understand.

4. Twenty-minute Plays involve the whole class in performing lines of text that becomes an express tour through the play. Early on, students learn and own the story and the language of the play and are motivated to keep reading. Folger Director of Education Peggy O'Brien originated this Essential and has perfected the art of finding the most fun-to-say lines in a play!

5. Choral Reading asks all students to read and reread a text aloud together. By changing what the "chorus" does in each rereading, this exercise gives students multiple opportunities to refine their understanding of the text. Students discover how the simple acts of speaking and rereading strengthen comprehension and analysis—all without any teacher explanation. In the chorus, there's an anonymity that's freeing, especially for English Learners and shy readers. Choral Reading is immersive, low-stakes, and really, really powerful.

6. 3D Lit enables a class or group of students to work together, figuring out (a) what is going on in a scene they have never before read with no explanation and very little help from you, and (b) how to informally act it out, making decisions as they go. This process enables them to refine their understanding as they transform the text from the page to a 3D "stage" in class. Michael Tolaydo, an actor, director, and faculty member of the Teaching Shakespeare Institute, created this groundbreaking Essential.

7. Cutting a Scene gets students close-reading with a purpose by challenging groups to eliminate half the lines from a piece of text while retaining its meaning. Since editors, scholars, directors, actors, and students have been cutting Shakespeare *forever*, yours are in good company. In fulfilling their mission as editors, students will naturally have to examine what the text says and implies, how the scene works, who's who, how language functions, and what's at stake. The fun part? Listening to your students debating which lines should stay or go and what the scene's "meaning" is anyway.

8. Promptbooks engage students in a process of text-based decision-making and collaborative annotation that reflects how they would stage a text. Many teachers and students call promptbooks "annotating with a real purpose." As with other Essentials, promptbooks are useful for students grappling with an unfamiliar text.

9. Group Scenes enable students to put all the pieces together. Students collaborate to select, cut, rehearse, memorize, and perform a scene for their classmates. Sometimes group scenes consist entirely of the original language of the text; other times they might include mashups or adaptations that incorporate home languages, pop culture, and/ or the wide world of literature. Students make their own Shakespeares, demonstrating how they have used textual evidence and background knowledge not only to understand but also reinvent complex dramatic language.

A Note on Differentiation

You know better than anyone else that inside every single one of your students is a whole lot of talent and a whole lot of room to improve. Therefore, when we talk about "differentiation," we are not talking about "struggling readers" or "remediation." We are talking about the rich diversity of what everyone brings to—and takes from—the learning. And everyone—*everyone*—has a great deal to bring and take!

So, are we talking about students in your AP or IB classes? Neurodiverse students? Students with IEPs? Nontraditional students? English Learners? So-called "high-fliers"? Yes. All of the above. In other words, differentiation is about hearing, seeing, challenging, supporting, and inspiring each unique learner.

When teachers experience the Folger Method for themselves, they often point out how differentiation is woven right into the Essentials. Because this mode of teaching relies so heavily on student voice, it is inherently personalized.

Beyond this general fact, though, there are several specific ways in which the Folger Method accounts for the variety of learners in your classroom. Allow us to zoom in on just two of them.

Example #1: The Essential called "Two-line Scenes" provides opportunities for students of all reading abilities to be successful. Each student works with a partner to make a "mini-play" from just two lines of Shakespeare. If, in one pair, Student A knows just two words in their assigned line, they can base their performance on those two words, or they can collaborate with their scene partner, Student B, to work out the meaning of the rest of their line. And if Student B knows not only the literal but also the figurative meaning of both lines, they can share their understanding with Student A and work together to take on the additional challenge of expressing subtext with their voices and bodies. Differentiation is happening on two fronts here: first, through the "wiggle room" that allows each student to bring their own knowledge and creativity to the final product (sometimes called "variable outcomes" by learning experts); second, through peer collaboration. Throughout this book, you will see that students are supporting and stretching each other, and developing their own independent thinking skills, thanks to all kinds of grouping configurations.

Example #2: Since much of the Folger Method relies on selecting and chunking text for our students, there is a ready-made structure for matching students with passages that meet them where they are and stretch them to the next level. In this book you will find that a relentless focus on language is one of the best tools you have for differentiating learning. In other words, don't change the task, water anything down, or make it overly complicated—just chunk the text into appropriately challenging parts. (If you teach English Learners and multilingual students—who are used to attending very carefully to language, its sound, its sense, its nuance—all this will strike you as familiar. For more on the unique power of the Folger Method with English Learners, turn to Dr. Christina Porter's excellent essay in this book.)

7 Touchstone Questions

As you jump into this book and these lessons, try using the following "Touchstone Questions" as your guide to reflecting on your own teaching. Think of them as a kind of checklist for student-driven, language-focused learning. Like everything else in this book, they are grounded in the 8 Foundational Principles.

If you can answer "yes" to each Touchstone Question, there must be some serious sparks flying in your classroom!

1. Did I, the teacher, get out of the way and let students own their learning?

2. Is the language of the text(s) front and center?

3. Are the words of the text in ALL students' mouths?

4. Are students collaborating to develop their own interpretations?

5. Are students daring to grapple with complex language and issues in the text?

6. Has every voice been included and honored?

7. Am I always giving students the real thing, whether it's Shakespeare's language, or primary sources, or supporting tough conversations as prompted by the text?

You've Got This

The Folger Method is proof of what's possible when we as teachers step back and let students own their learning. When we teachers realize we don't need to have all the answers. When students are invited to question and grapple. When they approach language with curiosity and care. When they tackle the real thing. When everyone tries new challenges, takes big risks, and supports one another along the way. When all students realize they can do hard things on their own.

You have everything you need to make this happen. We believe in you and can't wait to hear how it goes.

Othello Day-by-Day: The Five-Week Unit Plan

TEACHER-TO-TEACHER THOUGHTS AND THE GAME PLAN FOR THIS *OTHELLO*

Noelle Cammon and David A. Fulco

Teacher-to-Teacher Thoughts

Othello fully engages today's students like few other texts can. Characters that are influenced by the thoughts and reactions of others recall internet and social media culture. Characters that are fearful and jealous in relationships recall the drama of teenage love and school hallway disputes. Characters that listen to their friends over their own gut recall the peer pressure that is inherent in students who are growing and maturing. Characters that are forced to justify their worth in a society that doesn't value them recall the struggle that many students who are marginalized for one reason or another feel in our schools.

When you choose to teach *Othello* in your classroom, you are making a choice to confront, analyze, and discuss these problems in the play. Go for it! There is no workaround. You will find yourself in classroom conversations about peer pressure, alcoholism, abusive relationships, and yes, race and its role in society. While other Shakespeare plays touch on many of these issues, only *Othello* brings all of them to the forefront and demands that you face them head-on.

For the teacher, this means preparation and inner reflection. English class provides us with the opportunity to dive into a wide range of issues with our classes. And with *Othello*, every scene brings a new challenge and a new "touchy" subject to address with our students. It is a Shakespeare play that is difficult—not necessarily because of the language, but because of the way that the play forces us to confront our own prejudices and pushes us to listen to our students and to their lived experiences. Students lead, instead of the teacher dominating them with "theory" and "interpretation."

Race in *Othello* is often the toughest for educators and students to approach. It is hard to do this work because race remains an open wound in our nation. Although the news and media offer us almost daily reminders of the racial inequities in our country, many of us have not learned how to address this issue in authentic and meaningful ways. If our classrooms are microcosms of our larger society, then they are the places where we have the greatest opportunity to participate in the conversations that should lead to greater inclusivity and equity for all of our students, and to affect change.

It remains a challenge to teach *Othello* even for us, but we continue to take it on because it is a challenge that is worthy of our students. Students are ready to have these conversations. They are ready to engage with the problems of the world. When we choose Shakespeare, and we specifically choose *Othello,* we are telling our students that we want to hear from them and that we care about how they feel about the issues that have dogged society from Shakespeare's time to ours. *Othello* allows students to take this step because it demands our very best: as scholars, as teachers, and as citizens in our classroom communities.

The Folger Method allows both of us to have the discussions in class that are necessary when working through the play. Our lessons focus on Shakespeare's language in ways that allow students **to develop confidence and ease with "speaking Shakespeare."** It is the belief of the Folger that **Shakespeare is for EVERYONE,** and this means that we get Shakespeare's words into the mouth of every student beginning on Day 1. All students in your classroom can consider lines deeply, question the intention of dialogue, and—yes!—use movement as a close-reading strategy to get at the deeper meaning of the work.

The lessons included here give you permission to unburden yourself from teaching every line and every scene of *Othello.* Peggy O'Brien, the Folger's founding director of education and general editor of these *Teacher Guides,* says, "No one deserves a four-hour *Hamlet"* and we believe the same kind of thing about *Othello.* Therefore, the lessons here will work through specific scenes but not ALL the scenes. Included with our scenes are Shakespeare talk-backs, paired texts, contextual approaches to teaching about the history of the performance of the play, and conversations on race and relationships in the current day. We are not in the business of placing Shakespeare or his work on a pedestal; these lessons demand that we confront the problems with the play and the playwright while we continue to look inside ourselves.

In the end, it is the student who drives this unit of study. Students move through the Folger arc of learning—from word, to line, to speech, to scene, to play—in order to take ownership over the play. They will become masters of this close-reading technique and will be ready to lead discussion as they justify the choices that they make with their scene work and their performances. **Our lessons invite questioning, argument, and collaboration. They ask students to compare interpretations or performance choices and ground their final decisions in the text, because entertaining multiple interpretations knocks the idea of ONE *Othello* (or ONE way of understanding this play, or ONE way of understanding Shakespeare) and cracks the play and its writer wide open.**

From Noelle Cammon:

When I first started teaching, I began with a question: "Why teach Shakespeare at all?" While I love the Bard personally and studied the plays voraciously in college and grad school, I couldn't seem to translate that passion into teaching it.

I'd been teaching for twelve years by that time and had only had the chance to teach Shakespeare twice—once when I taught Julius Caesar *to some unsuspecting tenth graders and once when I taught* Romeo and Juliet *to my first set of ninth graders. Both of these attempts seemed like epic failures. I was so discouraged when my then-principal said, "All you really need to teach for* Julius Caesar *is just that one speech." As if "that one speech" was the only thing worth teaching. I felt a little more confident with* Romeo and Juliet. *I was at a new school and*

I had the help of some great teachers. I went for it! Students performed scenes from the play. They wrote Facebook and Twitter pages for their chosen characters. But even with all of these highly engaging activities, I felt like they missed key aspects of the play and only really gained a passable understanding of the plot. We worked on the play for eight to ten weeks and they came away with no real connection to it. So I asked the question: Doesn't there have to be something more socially and culturally relevant, something more worthwhile for my students to experience to justify all the time we had spent on this Shakespeare play?

And then I learned to use the Folger Method. It wasn't a magic wand. It was a key that helped me to open doors for my students. The Folger Method is messy. It's loud and it's disruptive and it follows the trajectory of the student, not the teacher. It gives students the ability and license to make meaningful connections to the text that are all their own. It lets me facilitate the journey without getting in their way. Most importantly, the Folger Method allows students to bring all of who they are to the reading of a text. Students have the agency to elevate Shakespeare to relevance instead of the other way around. And they make the most of that agency.

Almost as a by-product, using the Folger Method revealed how my own insecurities about teaching Shakespeare showed up in my expectations of students. Because it taught me to teach, it also taught me to believe in the unlimited brilliance of my students. For that, I will always be grateful to this work.

So why teach Shakespeare? Why teach Othello? *Because it's worth the time for students to get into the text. It's worth the energy for students to pick apart these words and feel empowered by the process. It's worth it to see students handle a text like* Othello *or any Shakespeare and make it their own.*

From David Fulco:

Each time I get ready to teach Othello, *I feel like I am teaching it for the first time. Because the issues in the play remain so relevant, I always feel that there are new news stories, media images, and articles that I can bring into my work with* Othello *to dig at the deeper meanings of the text.*

As a white educator working at a public school in New York City's South Bronx, I know that my students' experiences with race are greatly different from my own. I am always listening to and learning from my students, but I find this is even more important when working through Othello. *We are engaging with a play that uses the term "black" as a curse. The language is often hurtful and blunt: there is no sugar-coating Shakespeare's intentions when his Othello says, "I am black / And have not those soft parts of conversation."*

The class always rallies around each other during the reading of the play. Othello *is difficult, and students love a challenge, especially one that allows them to engage so easily in their own lived experiences. It is always the students that I look to when I am unsure. I trust in their intelligence, maturity, and morality. They want to have these conversations. And they want to engage in texts in a meaningful and authentic way without shying away from the societal truths that are presented.*

The world is a scary and messy place, and this is also true about teaching Othello. *The topics it surfaces never get any easier to deal with. What remains constant, however, are the students' reactions to the text, their deep understanding about what is right and wrong, and their commitment always to making the world a better place for all.*

Perhaps the best way of seeing all of this in action is with the culminating assessment for the unit—Week Five: a production of scenes and monologues from the play. Here students prove that Shakespeare's texts are three-dimensional—that they were written not to be studied at a desk, but to be performed on a stage for an audience! Students will decide on their own movement, props, sets, costumes, and interpretation as they put Othello *on its feet during Week Five. The energy during this week, moving from anxiety to joy, is the crowning testament to the community that you will have built during this unit. Students will feel empowered to have found success in something that they once thought impossible. And they will bring the close-reading exercises developed through the unit to the next complex text they encounter.*

It is an enormous challenge bringing Othello *into the classroom. The responsibility to the work and to Shakespeare himself can seem daunting. But it is important to remember that the only real responsibility you have during this unit is to your students. Trust them! And when all else fails, listen to your class. You don't need to have all the answers, but you'll find that giving space for the students to challenge the issues in the play will lead to full classroom engagement and the deep criticality that we all want in an English classroom.*

Although Iago tells us at the end of the play that "From this time forth, I never will speak a word," students will never forget their Othello *experience or the opportunity you afforded them—to bring their own voices and their whole selves to the work.*

The Game Plan for This *Othello*

The overview chart below outlines five weeks of lessons for working through *Othello*. The lessons explore Acts 1 through 5, leading up to a performance on the last day of the unit of student-selected scenes from the play. The lessons are NOT exhaustive. The scenes included were chosen to reflect the greatest opportunity for student engagement, analysis, and current connections to the material. Identity takes center stage in these lessons, and the students should find time to reflect on their own identity as Othello's identity succumbs to manipulation and descends into chaos.

Due to the difficult nature of reading a Shakespearean text, these lessons were written to be completed in a 45-minute class. If homework is an important aspect of your school culture, we suggest assigning articles, news clips, political cartoons, or online videos that relate to the larger themes and issues presented in the play. Allowing students to see that the "problems" we like to point to in the text are still problems today is a sobering reminder that the work for social equity is not over and that perhaps we haven't come as far as we think from the early 17th century.

The procedure for each lesson is called "What Students Hear (From You) and (Then What They'll) Do." In that section of each lesson, we've written instructions for what you will say (thus, what students hear) and what you will see students do as the lesson proceeds. It's as close as we can get to inviting you into our classrooms to watch and listen as a lesson unfolds. In some places, we have shared any additional "teacher thoughts" that should factor into the work in a [**TEACHER NOTE**.] The lessons close with "Here's What Just Happened in Class," so you can get a sense of what students learned and what skills they practiced over the course of the lesson. Teaching colleagues suggested that we add this section because, as they said, "sometimes when you're teaching in a completely new way, you can't tell exactly what's going on!"

DAY-BY-DAY

Week/Act	Questions Guiding Exploration of the Play:	Lessons:
Week One	Who is Othello—what do others say? What does HE say?	**1.** Shakespeare in Context **2.** "But words are words" meet *Othello:* Tossing Lines and Two-Line Scenes **3.** "To love the Moor": Putting *Othello* 1.1 on Its Feet **4.** "I follow him to serve my turn upon him": Putting 1.1 on Its Feet **5.** "I do perceive here a divided duty": Desdemona and what is "owed"
Week Two	Othello as a construct and symbol—blackness as a construct	**6.** "Speaking for myself": Close-Reading Othello's Defense **7.** "Put on your poker face, Brotha . . .": *American Moor* talks to *Othello* **8.** "Will be tenderly led by the nose": Exploring Iago's plan through soliloquies in 1.3 and 2.1 **9.** "Reputation, reputation, reputation!": Cutting in *Othello* 2.3 **10.** "Speak. Who began this?": Cut to Performance in *Othello* 2.3
Week Three	Manipulation of characters (Desdemona, Cassio, Othello) and hard truths	**11.** "Peevish Jealousies": Tone, Emphasis, and Proximity **12.** "Why Did I Marry?": Othello and Desdemona's Relationship (3.3) **13.** "There's magic in the web of it": What's up with that handkerchief? **14.** "By heaven, you do me wrong": Exploring jealousy through Essentials promptbooks **15.** "Alas, what ignorant sin have I committed?": Exploring jealousy through your promptbooks and 3D Lit

Week Four	What do we make of the end of the play? Emilia speaks with Lucille Clifton.	**16.** "The Ills We Do, Their Ills Instruct Us So": Emilia and Lucille Clifton in Conversation **17.** "O, I Am Spoiled, Undone by Villains": Identity and Image **18.** "And Smote Him, Thus": A 20-Minute Act 5 **19.** "To Die Upon a Kiss": Determining Identity Through Othello's Final Monologues **20.** "This Heavy Act With Heavy Heart Relate": Whose Tragedy Is It Anyway?
Week Five	How will WE tell the rest of this story together? How does the text guide our decisions?	**21.** Your Final Projects! **22–24.** Your Final Project: Making *Othello* Your Own **25.** The Final Project: Your Own *Othello*, Performed!

WEEK ONE: LESSON 1

Shakespeare in Context

Here's What We're Doing and Why

As students begin their study, they will be bringing with them their past experiences with Shakespeare and their preconceived notions about his work. Today we'll take a minute to allow your students to discover that the universe of Shakespeare is bigger, more diverse, and more interesting than they may realize. This lesson is all about giving everyone a taste of context—a brief glimpse into some of the most expansive, exciting, and surprising aspects of studying Shakespeare, his words, and his world. It zooms out way beyond *Othello* for a moment!

By the end of this lesson, students will have examined their own ideas about Shakespeare's world. They will have enlarged their sense of history by studying four primary-source documents and a single 21st-century one, spanning the 1600s to the 1900s. They will have reflected on the wide world of Shakespeare and their place in it.

What Will I Need?

- Portrait of Abd el-Ouahed ben Messaoud ben Mohammed Anoun, Moroccan Ambassador to Queen Elizabeth I, ca. 1600 – **RESOURCE #1.1A**

- John Smith's Map of Virginia and the Chesapeake, a 1631 copy of the 1612 original – **RESOURCE #1.1B**

- Portraits by Wenceslaus Hollar, 1645 – **RESOURCE #1.1C**

- Broadside publicizing Ira Aldridge's First Appearance at Covent Garden as Othello, 1833 – **RESOURCE #1.1D**

- *Romeo y Julieta*, "Prologo," Pablo Neruda, written in 1964, published in 2001 – **RESOURCE #1.1E**

- 6 Mind-blowing Facts about Shakespeare and History – **RESOURCE #1.1F**

- Large paper, markers, and/or Post-it notes for the gallery walk we're calling "Document Speed Dating"

How Should I Prepare?

- Set up your classroom for "Document Speed Dating":
  - Post the five documents at various stations around the room. Make sure the images are big and clear enough for everyone to see details and there's enough space around each document for students to respond in writing.
  - You can use whiteboards, butcher paper, or Post-it notes—just make sure that there's room for everyone to "talk back" to each image.

- Organize your students into five groups, each one starting at a different station.

Agenda (one 45-minute class)

- ❏ Prior Knowledge Free Write: 7 minutes
- ❏ Speed Dating Instructions: 3 minutes
- ❏ Speed Dating Exercise: 21 minutes
- ❏ The List: 6 minutes
- ❏ Reflection Round: 8 minutes

Here's What Students Hear (From You) and (Then What They'll) Do

Part One: Prior Knowledge Free Write

1. Jot down your thoughts on any of the following questions. When you imagine the world of Shakespeare, what do you see? What images come to your mind? Who are the people? What do they look and sound like? What are the places and objects? What's the vibe?

   Turn to a classmate and discuss what each of you wrote.

   As a class, we'll share the images and ideas that arose in the paired conversations. [**TEACHER NOTE:** Record student responses on the board in a broad way—no need to be exhaustive here. The point is to capture things like "people in ruffs and crowns" or "outdoor theatres" or "white Europeans" or "candlelight and quills" or "street fighting" or "plague" or "boring" or "lively" or "smelly clothes" or "harp music"—whatever comes to your students' minds. **Welcome all responses without editorializing.**]

Part Two: Document Speed Dating

Now you are going to meet actual historical documents from the world of Shakespeare. Your job is to:

   a. Look very closely at what you see.

   b. Write down your observations right alongside the document.

   c. Keeping in mind your earlier impressions of Shakespeare's world, what in each image jumps out at you? What do you wonder about?

[**TEACHER NOTE:** You can keep the "What in the image jumps out at you?" prompt posted for students to see throughout this exercise.]

   d. Get into your groups and begin at your assigned station. Each group should be at a different station.

   e. You will have roughly 3 minutes at each station. As a group, move to the next station when you hear "Next!" Continue until every group has studied and written observations about all five documents.

   f. Now that everyone has gone on a "speed date" with each document, return to your seat and find a partner.

With this partner, discuss the main things that jumped out at you in these documents. Did anything surprise you? Did you learn anything new about the world of Shakespeare? We'll share more as a whole class in a few moments . . .

Part Three: The List

Let's look at the list of "6 Mind-blowing Facts about Shakespeare and History." – **RESOURCE #1.5F.**

[**TEACHER NOTE:** Call for six volunteers to read each fact aloud. Save discussion for the reflection round below.]:

Part Four: Reflection Round

1. Now it's time for each of you to share your reflections on today's learning. We'll do two rounds. Remember, just one sentence from each student and not more at this point. We want to hear from EVERY voice!

2. First, finish the sentence, "Something that changed my original mental picture of Shakespeare's world was . . ."

3. Second, finish the sentence, "I am still wondering . . ."

4. In closing, can you summarize the main ways in which these documents have enlarged or transformed your understanding of Shakespeare's world? Individually? As a class?

Here's What Just Happened in Class:

- Students have identified and interrogated their prior knowledge—and assumptions—of Shakespeare's world.

- Students have examined five different documents spanning four centuries in order to enlarge their understanding of Shakespeare and history. They have seen for themselves that Shakespeare's Britain was multicultural and very much connected to the Americas.

- Students know important and surprising facts about the wide world of Shakespeare.

RESOURCE #1.1A

Abd el-Ouahed ben Messaoud ben Mohammed Anoun,
Ambassador from Morocco to the court of Queen Elizabeth I,
beginning in 1600

RESOURCE #1.1B

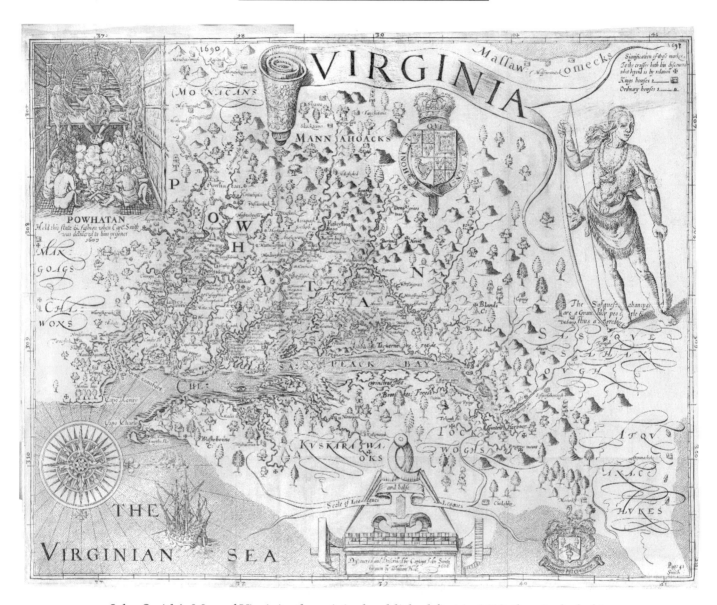

John Smith's Map of Virginia, the original published first in 1612, then included in the first edition of his book that was published in 1624. His book was popular—this image map is copied from the second edition of his book, published in 1631.

RESOURCE #1.1C

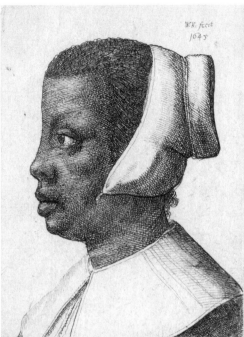

Portraits by Wenceslaus Hollar, made in and around 1645

RESOURCE #1.1D

Ira Aldridge's First Appearance at Covent Garden as Othello

RESOURCE #1.1E

PROLOGO

ENTRA EL CORO

CORO
En la bella Verona esto sucede:
dos casas ambas en nobleza iguales
con odio antiguo hacen discordia nueva.
La sangre tiñe sus civiles manos.

Dos horas durará en nuestro escenario esta historia: escuchadla con paciencia, suplirá nuestro esfuerzo lo que falte.

Romeo y Julieta, Pablo Neruda, written 1964,
published 2001, "Prologo"

RESOURCE #1.1F

6 Mind-blowing Facts about Shakespeare and History

1. There were many people of different ethnicities and religions in Shakespeare's Britain. An important facet of this history: Africans participated in life at many social levels. Many were baptized—Protestant parishes retain the records. Black citizens included merchants, silk weavers, seamstresses, shoemakers, a circumnavigator who sailed with Sir Francis Drake, and a royal musician.

2. During her coronation festivities in 1600, Queen Elizabeth I entertained a large delegation of Muslim African officials, including Moroccan Ambassador Abd el-Ouahed ben Messaoud ben Mohammed Anoun. He returned to court often and served as her advisor. Some think that Shakespeare might have seen him and other African diplomats at court and drawn inspiration from them.

3. William Shakespeare was writing plays as English settlers colonized Jamestown, Virginia, in 1607. It's generally thought that he based his play *The Tempest* on accounts of a well-known shipwreck that occurred off the coast of Bermuda. The ship was called *Sea Venture* and it was on its way to Jamestown.

4. Ira Aldridge was the first Black man and African American actor to play the role of Othello at a professional theater: the Theatre Royal, Covent Garden, London, in 1833. Born in New York City, Aldridge performed Shakespeare all over Europe because as a Black man, he could not have done so in America. He was perhaps the first American star of the international Shakespeare stage. More than 100 years later in 1943, Paul Robeson was only the second Black actor to play Othello in the United States—on Broadway.

5. It was not until 1660 that the first woman actor performed Shakespeare onstage. Until then, men and boys had played all the parts. At this point, though, women took on not just female characters, but also male characters.

6. Shakespeare's works have been adapted and performed around the globe for centuries, and they have been translated into over 100 languages.

WEEK ONE: LESSON 2

"But words are words"
Meet *Othello*: Tossing Lines and Two-Line Scenes

Here's What We're Doing Today and Why

This week is all about getting familiar with *Othello* the play and Othello the character. Students need to know immediately that our study of Shakespeare will be rooted deeply in the language. The plots can be fun and/or exciting, sure, but we read Shakespeare for the language.

In this lesson, students will get to know *Othello*—the play and the man—through language. We'll use two of the Folger Essentials: Tossing Lines and Two-Lines Scenes. Both activities get Shakespeare's words in students' mouths while providing a low-risk way for students to become familiar with the text. And they get students thinking and creating with the language and taking risks. It also gets you, the teacher, out of the way, allowing the students to explore the text on their own and come up with their own interpretations and expectations of the text. We end with a reflection that will have students considering how they themselves relate to our play.

Today, students are in the driver's seat. They will read, they will speak, and they will analyze *Othello* together and lay the groundwork for all the work to come.

[**TEACHER NOTE:** In this lesson, students will grapple with some pejorative language that is offensive but is nonetheless part of this text. We have purposely not removed it, but we are aware that such pejorative language has been and still is a hurtful insult to African Americans and darker-skinned persons of other racial and ethnic groups when used by those who are not African American or darker-skinned people. We feel that we cannot ignore this language, and neither can we skirt conversation about it because doing so allows the hate and prejudice of that language to fester and perpetuate. You know your students. Students' feelings and reactions to words depend on many factors, including demographics. Please take the time to handle with care conversations and questions that may come up.]

Agenda (45-minute period)

- ❏ Part One—Tossing Lines: 10 minutes
- ❏ Part Two—Two-Line Scenes: 25 minutes
- ❏ Part Three—Reflection Rounds: 10 minutes

What Will I Need?

- Two-line line cards – **RESOURCE #1.2** at the end of this lesson
- Some beanbags/balled-up socks or anything soft that can be thrown safely

How Should I Prepare?

- PRINT and CUT OUT the *Othello* line cards.

- Arrange your classroom so that all students can be seen (circle, semicircle); move desks and tables out of the way if possible.

Here's What Students Hear (From You) and (Then What They'll) Do

Part One: Tossing Lines

1. Choose a line from the stack of line cards.

2. Read your line to yourself three times. Now read it out loud.

[**TEACHER NOTE:** Resist the temptation to define words or correct pronunciation. You may want to share with students that we were not there when Shakespeare wrote these words and so we do not know for sure how to pronounce them either.]

3. Move around the room and read your line aloud over and over. As you move, play with the tone and stress of different words in the line. Change your volume each time you read.

4. Now let's make a circle of five or six people. I'll give each circle one beanbag or soft toy.

5. "Toss" lines within each circle by tossing a beanbag to one another and saying your lines in different ways each time you catch the beanbag. Make sure that everyone in the circle speaks before anyone gets the beanbag twice. Toss lines as many times as you can before I call for us all to stop.

6. Now, let's make a big circle with the whole class.

7. Without the beanbag, let's share lines from person to person around the circle. Then repeat by going around the circle a second time in the opposite direction.

8. Discuss in the circle:

   What did you think of all that?

   What kind of world do you think we're about to enter as we begin *Othello*?

   What gives you that idea?

   What else do you notice about the words or lines you just shared?

Part Two: Two-Lines Scenes

1. Now, let's do something else with these lines: Move around the room saying your line again. When I say "stop," find a partner closest to you. With your partner, you have 5 minutes to create and rehearse a scene that uses only your two lines. Think about how you say your line and maybe some physical action too.

2. Form a big circle again; it's time to perform your scene! When it's your turn, step forward with your partner and perform your scene after the class "counts

you in." Together, the class chants "3 . . . 2 . . . 1 . . . action!," then you and your partner perform your two-line scene.

3. When you finish your scene, take a bow while the class applauds wildly!

Part Three: Reflection Rounds

1. Stay in your big circle. To conclude today's lesson, respond to the following question with a word or one short sentence. We'll go around the circle so everyone can answer.

I noticed . . .

I wondered . . .

[**TEACHER NOTE:** If responses stay focused on the language and activities, you should add: Something I learned about myself was . . .]

Here's What Just Happened in Class

- Shakespeare's words were in students' mouths.

- Students collaborated with one another and got familiar with keywords and juicy lines from *Othello*.

- Students' voices were amplified and they made decisions about how to interpret the text.

- You got out of the way and allowed students to do all of this on their own.

RESOURCE #1.2

Othello Line Cards

Mere prattle without practice is all his soldiership	I follow him to serve my turn upon him.
In following him I follow but myself.	An old black ram is tupping your white ewe.
Where may we apprehend her and the Moor?	Her father loved me, oft invited me.
She gave me for my pains a world of kisses.	She loved me for the dangers I had passed.
If virtue no delighted beauty lack, Your son-in-law is far more fair than black.	Put money in thy purse.
News, lads! Our wars are done.	With as little a web as this will I ensnare as great a fly as Cassio.
Didst thou not see her paddle with the palm of his hand?	That Cassio loves her, I do well believe it.
I do suspect the lusty Moor hath leapt into my seat.	Never more be officer of mine.
O, I have lost my reputation!	I will beseech the virtuous Desdemona to undertake for me.
Cassio, I will do all my abilities in thy behalf.	Was not that Cassio parted from my wife?
When I love thee not, chaos is come again.	O, beware, my lord, of jealousy.
No, Iago, I'll see before I doubt.	Look to your wife. Observe her well with Cassio.
Why did I marry?	I am abused, and my relief must be to loathe her.
I am glad I have found this napkin.	The Moor already changes with my poison.
'Twas I that killed her.	What should such a fool do with so good a wife?

It is their husbands' faults if wives do fall.	Are not you a strumpet?
I have not deserved this.	What ignorant sin have I committed?
Strangle her in her bed.	Confess? Handkerchief? O devil!
There's magic in the web of it.	Give me a living reason she's disloyal.

"To Love the Moor": Putting *Othello* 1.1 on Its Feet

Here's What We're Doing and Why

You'll recall that our focus this week is on getting to know *Othello* the play and Othello the character. In the last lesson, students worked with the language of the play and made predictions about potential conflicts and problems within the play. The language was in students' mouths and there was a general, if-sketchy-in-places, understanding about what is to come in the play.

Today, students get the opportunity to put the language in context. Across these next two class periods, students will closely read and perform Act 1, scene 1 of *Othello* using the Folger Essentials Choral Reading and 3D Lit. Starting a Shakespeare unit by asking students to stage a scene might seem like dumping a beginning swimmer into the deep end of the pool, but you'll be surprised how quickly students learn to "float," and how the problem-solving and critical thinking that students practice in this activity prepare them for close-reading of other scenes. At times, it's going to feel like organized chaos in your classroom, and that's okay. The point is for students to use the text to lead the decisions they make about the scene.

The work today with students will pay dividends in your classroom. The lessons will show students that they have the power to read and understand Shakespeare with very little help from you. The text that students will use is a scene that has been cut to focus on action and dialogue that double as stage directions, allowing students to plunge headfirst into the work. They will be working together to understand the many aspects of the scene and then will have an opportunity to perform it. This is the first step for students toward their final performances at the end of the unit.

What Will I Need?

- Copies of *Othello* Act 1, scene 1, edited, for each student – **RESOURCE #1.3**

How Should I Prepare?

- Arrange your classroom so that all students can be seen (circle, semicircle); move desks and tables out of the way if possible.

Agenda (one 45-minute class period)

❏ Part One: Read and Own the Scene: 45 minutes

Here's What Students Hear (From You) and (Then What They'll) Do

Part One: Read and Own the Scene

1. Okay, everyone, let's sit in a circle. Each of you has your own copy of the scene and a pencil.

2. Let's read the scene aloud, together in one voice. Read quickly and loudly; try to stay on pace with the group.

3. Share your level of understanding on a scale of 1 to 10, 10 meaning "I understand everything" and 1 meaning "Huh? What?" Hold up your fingers or shout out your number.

4. Let's read the text again, this time sequentially, around the circle person to person. Each person reads to an end punctuation—a period, a semicolon, a colon, a question mark, or an exclamation point, and then the next reader takes over. Readers do not change at a comma—read through a comma.)

[**TEACHER NOTE:** Depending on how it goes, you may want to do this round twice. Sometimes it takes a minute to get the end punctuation breaks.]

5. So . . . good job! And here are some questions:

   a. Who are these people? And how do you know this from the text?

   b. What is going on here? How do you know that from the text?

   c. Where are they? How do you know that from the text?

[**TEACHER NOTE:** Resist the urge to correct or editorialize so students make their own meaning from textual references. Give them time to find the answers in the text.]

6. Let's read it again another way: this time sequentially again, person-by-person, but each of you will read a character's whole speech, and then the person next to you takes the next character's speech. We'll change readers at the end of each character's speech.

7. Good job on this too. More of the same kinds of questions:

   a. What else do you notice about these people? Any new things? Where do you find that in the text?

   b. How do they feel about each other? Does the text give you any clues on that?

8. Let's read like we did last time, character by character, and this time let's mark up words or phrases or ideas you don't fully understand.

9. After this reading, we'll talk through what everybody marked up and we'll decide together about what the unfamiliar words and phrases mean.

10. Good job with this reading too. Let's hear the words and ideas that you're not sure about. [**TEACHER NOTE:** Students collaborate on figuring the meaning of words based on the context. They will be able to get further than you think! Send them to a dictionary or a phone only as a last resort.]

11. Now that we've worked through this scene in all of these ways, I'm going to ask about your level of understanding again: On a scale of 1 to 10, 10 meaning "I understand everything" and 1 meaning "Huh? What?," where do you think you are in understanding this piece of text? How about these questions:

    a. Is your number higher than it was when we started? [**TEACHER NOTE:** It will be, for sure.]

    b. What do you understand now that you didn't understand before?

    c. What do you think contributed to that understanding?

12. Hang on to your scripts, because we're going to do some fancy stuff with this scene in class tomorrow!

Here's What Just Happened in Class

- Students discovered the plot, setting, characters, and conflict in 1.1, pretty much all by themselves.

- Students worked through the scene in several different ways.

- Students increased their level of understanding from the beginning of class to the end.

- Students, without you really telling them anything, usually have figured this much out:
  - This Othello guy is in trouble.
  - Rodrigo, Iago, and Brabantio all have it out for Othello.
  - Rodrigo is angry that Othello has married the woman he loves.
  - Iago is angry and vengeful because Othello gave someone else the job he wanted.
  - Brabantio is angry that Othello has run away with his daughter.
  - Rodrigo, with the help of Iago, raises the alarm to Brabantio that Othello has run off with his daughter.

Othello 1.1, edited

RODERIGO

Thou toldst me thou didst hold him in thy hate.

IAGO

Despise me
If I do not. Three great ones of the city,
In personal suit to make me his lieutenant,
Off-capped to him; and, by the faith of man,
I know my price, I am worth no worse a place.
For "Certes," says he,
"I have already chose my officer."
And what was he?
One Michael Cassio, a Florentine,
That never set a squadron in the field,
Nor the division of a battle knows
Mere prattle without practice
Is all his soldiership. But he, sir, had th' election;
And I, of whom his eyes had seen the proof
At Rhodes, at Cyprus, and on other grounds
Christened and heathen, must be beeled and calmed

RODERIGO

By heaven, I rather would have been his hangman.
I would not follow him, then.

IAGO

O, sir, content you.
I follow him to serve my turn upon him.
We cannot all be masters, nor all masters
Cannot be truly followed. You shall mark
For, sir, it is as sure as you are Roderigo,
Were I the Moor I would not be Iago.
In following him, I follow but myself.
Heaven is my judge, not I for love and duty,
But seeming so for my peculiar end.
I am not what I am.

RODERIGO

What a full fortune does the thick-lips owe
If he can carry 't thus!

IAGO

Call up her father.
Rouse him. Make after him, poison his delight.

RODERIGO

Here is her father's house. I'll call aloud.
What ho, Brabantio! Signior Brabantio, ho!

IAGO

Awake! What ho, Brabantio! Thieves, thieves!
Look to your house, your daughter, and your bags!
Thieves, thieves!

BRABANTIO

What is the reason of this terrible summons?
What is the matter there?

RODERIGO

Signior, is all your family within?

BRABANTIO

Why, wherefore ask you this?

IAGO

Zounds, sir, you're robbed.
Even now, now, very now, an old black ram
Is tupping your white ewe. Arise, arise!
Awake the snorting citizens with the bell,
Or else the devil will make a grandsire of you.
Arise, I say!

BRABANTIO

What, have you lost your wits?

RODERIGO

Most reverend signior, do you know my voice?

BRABANTIO

Not I. What are you?

RODERIGO

My name is Roderigo.

BRABANTIO

In honest plainness thou hast heard me say
my daughter is not for thee.

IAGO

I am one, sir, that comes to tell you your daughter
and the Moor are now making the beast with
two backs.

BRABANTIO

Thou art a villain.

IAGO

You are a senator.

BRABANTIO

This thou shalt answer. I know thee, Roderigo.

RODERIGO

Sir, I will answer anything. But I beseech you,
If 't be your pleasure and most wise consent—
As partly I find it is—that your fair daughter,
At this odd-even and dull watch o' th' night,
Transported with no worse nor better guard
But with a knave of common hire, a gondolier,
To the gross clasps of a lascivious Moor:
If this be known to you, and your allowance,
We then have done you bold and saucy wrongs.
Your daughter, if you have not given her leave,
I say again, hath made a gross revolt,
Tying her duty, beauty, wit, and fortunes
In an extravagant and wheeling stranger
Of here and everywhere. Straight satisfy yourself.
If she be in her chamber or your house,
Let loose on me the justice of the state
For thus deluding you.

BRABANTIO

Strike on the tinder, ho! Call up all my people.

IAGO

Farewell, for I must leave you.
It seems not meet nor wholesome to my place
To be produced, as if I stay I shall,
Against the Moor.
That you shall surely find him,
Lead to the Sagittary the raisèd search,
And there will I be with him. So, farewell.

BRABANTIO

It is too true an evil. Gone she is,

With the Moor, sayst thou?—
Are they married, think you?

RODERIGO

Truly, I think they are.

BRABANTIO

O heaven! How got she out? O treason of the blood!
Fathers, from hence trust not your daughters' minds
By what you see them act.

RODERIGO

Yes, sir, I have indeed.

BRABANTIO

—O, would you had had her!—
Some one way, some another.—Do you know
Where we may apprehend her and the Moor?

RODERIGO

I think I can discover him, if you please
To get good guard and go along with me.

BRABANTIO

Pray you lead on. At every house I'll call.
I may command at most.—Get weapons, ho!
And raise some special officers of night.—
On, good Roderigo. I will deserve your pains.

"I Follow Him To Serve My Turn Upon Him": Putting *Othello* 1.1 on Its Feet

Here's What We're Doing Today and Why

The previous lesson focused on owning the language and making new discoveries about the text. Now it's time to use those discoveries to put the scene on its feet. Again, it's going to feel like organized chaos in your classroom, and that's okay.

For this next portion of the lesson, a few students will be actors and the rest of the class will become directors. Our role as teachers is to facilitate the directors' work. Get out of the way as much as you can. This is not at all about creating a product; rather, it engages all students in the process of learning about a scene and some of the many possible variations in this scene and in all of Shakespeare.

The teacher should not direct. Student directors do this work because they learn a tremendous amount about the variations possible in staging Shakespeare. This Folger Essential—3D Lit—is all about this process and what students discover and learn in that process. It has almost nothing to do with the product—the scene they end up with. It's all about what they learn through this process. We know we already said that, but it bears repeating!

As you move through the next steps, remember that any time the directors make suggestions or decisions, they should be prompted to *support their decisions with evidence from the text.*

What Will I Need?

- Copies of *Othello* Act 1, scene 1, edited – **RESOURCE #1.3**. These should be the ones students marked up during the previous lesson.

How Should I Prepare?

- Arrange your classroom so that all students can be seen (circle, semicircle); move desks and tables out of the way if possible

Agenda (one 45-minute class period)

❏ Part One—Putting the Scene on Its Feet: 35 minutes

❏ Part Two—Discussion and Reflection: 10 minutes

Here's What Students Hear (From You) and (Then What They'll) Do

Part One: Putting the Scene on Its Feet

1. Let's create a space so we can stage the scene.

One or two of you will serve as stage managers who write down the directors' ideas and stage directions that are tried out, and other decisions about playing the scene. Who will do that?

2. I'm going to cast who plays Brabantio, Iago, and Roderigo.

[**TEACHER NOTE:** Your sensibilities about your students are the best. The actors can only speak the words that Shakespeare gives them. The other students are directors, and they are the ones who make suggestions about how the actors should move, speak, emote, etc.]

3. Bring your actors to the "stage." All the students who are not acting are directors. No one sits out. Since there are only three actors, you might want to assign a specific group of directors to each actor.

4. Directors make decisions about the set and they "build" the set with objects found in the classroom.

   – Are there any props, furniture, or features necessary?

   – Where are the entrances and exits?

   – Does the text give you any clues on this?

5. Directors place the actors in their positions for the start of the scene.

6. Actors begin running the first few lines of the scene (a good chunk to start with is lines 1 to 7).

7. Based on their deep dive into the text in the previous class, directors will share what they noticed, what they feel needs to change, and what might be missing.

[**TEACHER NOTE:** Some details our classes often need to review:

• What time is it? Where are the characters? How do we know, and how can we perform that?

• Why are these two meeting? What's Rodrigo's attitude toward Iago? How do we know? How can the actor perform that?

• Check on the set—do any adjustments need to be made?]

8. Start the scene again and keep going. Throughout, directors can pause the scene when they see a change that needs to be made, always supporting their changes with evidence from the text.

9. Repeat this "run the scene/pause for redirection/rerun the lines" process until the scene closes or your end-of-class bell nears.

Part Two: Reflection

To conclude, perform these rounds by finishing these sentences:

• I observed . . .

• I was surprised . . .

Here's What Just Happened in Class

- Students discovered more about the plot, setting, characters, and conflict in 1.1.

- Students used Shakespeare's text to make decisions about their scenes.

- Students became familiar with an unfamiliar scene, took it off the page, and directed themselves on how to stage it.

- Students deepened their understanding of 1.1 by taking on the roles of actors, directors, and audience.

- Students did all of this with very little direction from you. This is students taking charge of their own learning and beginning to own Shakespeare.

"I Do Perceive Here a Divided Duty": Desdemona and What Is "Owed"

Here's What We're Doing Today and Why

Much of *Othello* focuses on the relationships between characters. Students have already looked at how outsiders view the relationship between Othello and "the gentle Desdemona," but we have not had an opportunity to meet her or to hear about their love from the characters themselves.

Today, students will explore the character of Desdemona through a monologue and scene work. Desdemona finds herself pulled between her husband, Othello, and her father, Brabantio. Students are already familiar with Brabantio's negative feelings toward Othello and Othello's deep love for Desdemona. However, this is the first time in the play that we have had the opportunity to hear directly from Desdemona about her thoughts on the role she plays in her family and the role she plays as a wife. Students will consider options and make supported observations about the overall character of Desdemona and the pressures placed upon her by her society.

The questions posed in this scene continue to relate to students today: What do I owe my parents? What do I owe my significant other/friends? As students close-read, they will be able to engage in these personal connections and consider how their own experiences are reflected in the actions and feelings of Desdemona. As students explore the dialogue and the conflicts in today's scenes, they are diving deep into some of the most important aspects of the play—loyalty, individuality, and societal expectations.

What Will I Need?

- Copies of *Othello* 1.3.208–218 – **RESOURCE #1.5A**
- Copies of *Othello* 1.3.268–343 – **RESOURCE #1.5B**

Agenda (one 45-minute period)

- ❏ Part One—Review and Warm-up: Where are we in the play? (5 minutes)
- ❏ Part Two—Choral Reading of Desdemona Monologue 1.3.208–218 (10 minutes)
- ❏ Part Three—Scene Work between Desdemona, Brabantio, and Othello (25 minutes)
- ❏ Part Four—Reflection (either written individually or discussed generally) (5 minutes)

Here's What Students Hear (From You) and (Then What They'll) Do

Part One: Review/Warm-up

Brabantio asks Desdemona, "Do you perceive in all this noble company where you most owe obedience?"

    a. What do you think he means?

    b. How does one "owe obedience" to another?

    c. Have you ever felt torn between what you owe to two different people?

Part Two: Choral Reading—Desdemona Monologue, *Othello* 1.3.208–218

1. Let's read this short speech like we have read others in previous lessons. Read the speech as loud and fast as you can while still staying together with the rest of the class.

2. Let's read it again, loud and fast, and think about how you feel when you must defend yourself. Read it that way.

3. By a different show of fingers (1 = "I'm lost," 3 = "I've got this!"), indicate your understanding of the speech.

4. Next, how about two volunteers read the speech by reading alternating lines? The first starts out "My noble father," the second "I do perceive here a divided duty."

5. What do you notice about this speech? What do you hear?

6. What do you think Desdemona is thinking about or feeling? How do you know?

7. After this reading, check again for understanding using the finger system. If more students are holding up two fingers, ask, "What more did you notice about the speech in this reading?" Remind students to point out words or lines in the speech that help them to develop their answers.

8. Questions:
   - What questions do you have?
   - What's happening here? How do you know?
   - How does Desdemona feel about Brabantio? Othello? How do you know?
   - Do you sympathize with Desdemona?
   - Who has the power in this scene?
   - Is there conflict? If there is, what's causing it? Is it inevitable?
   - What do you now know about Desdemona that you didn't know before?

Part Three: Desdemona and Brabantio and *Othello*, 1.3.268–343

1. Have a look at this script, 1.3.268–343.

2. Let's read sequentially around the circle, speakers changing at each end punctuation mark. What is going on here? What does the text tell you?

3. Read the scene again, this time in parts.

4. What has been decided in this scene? Do you feel like this is the right decision?

Part Four: Reflection (either written individually or discussed generally): Reflect on what we just read and talked about:

- What is your understanding of Desdemona after reading this scene?

- Have you had moments of conflict like this with your family or other authority figures in your life? What were the consequences of moments like this?

- Other observations on this scene and what's going on here?

Here's What Just Happened in Class

- Students took a deep dive into the language from and about Desdemona—and this resulted in a deeper understanding of her character.

- Students, by their own investigation, learned that Desdemona has agency in the play but that she feels the weight of making decisions that might disappoint others.

- Students, as always, supported their work with evidence from the text.

- Students made a personal connection with Desdemona and had a chance to think about the role that expectations can have in their own lives.

RESOURCE #1.5A

Othello 1.3.208–218

DESDEMONA

  My noble father,
  I do perceive here a divided duty.
  To you I am bound for life and education.   210
  My life and education both do learn me
  How to respect you. You are the lord of duty.
  I am hitherto your daughter. But here's my
    husband.

  And so much duty as my mother showed   215
  To you, preferring you before her father,
  So much I challenge that I may profess
  Due to the Moor my lord.

Othello 1.3.268–343, edited

OTHELLO
Most humbly, therefore, bending to your state,
I crave fit disposition for my wife,
Due reference of place and exhibition,
With such accommodation and besort
As levels with her breeding.

DUKE Why, at her father's.

BRABANTIO I will not have it so.

OTHELLO Nor I.

DESDEMONA
Nor would I there reside
To put my father in impatient thoughts
By being in his eye. Most gracious duke,
To my unfolding lend your prosperous ear
And let me find a charter in your voice
T' assist my simpleness.

DUKE What would you, Desdemona?

DESDEMONA
That I love the Moor to live with him
My downright violence and storm of fortune
May trumpet to the world. My heart's subdued
Even to the very quality of my lord.
I saw Othello's visage in his mind,
And to his honors and his valiant parts
Did I my soul and fortunes consecrate.
So that, dear lords, if I be left behind,
A moth of peace, and he go to the war,
The rites for why I love him are bereft me
And I a heavy interim shall support
By his dear absence. Let me go with him.

OTHELLO
Let her have your voice.

DUKE

    Be it as you shall privately determine,
    Either for her stay or going. Th' affair cries haste,
    And speed must answer it.

(FIRST) SENATOR You must away tonight.

OTHELLO With all my heart.

DUKE

    Let it be so.
    Good night to everyone.

(TO BRABANTIO) And, noble signior,
    If virtue no delighted beauty lack,
    Your son-in-law is far more fair than black.

(FIRST) SENATOR

    Adieu, brave Moor, use Desdemona well.

BRABANTIO

    Look to her, Moor, if thou hast eyes to see.
    She has deceived her father, and may thee.

OTHELLO My life upon her faith!

"Speaking for Myself": Close-Reading Othello's Defense

Here's What We're Doing Today and Why

This week is all about the "construction" of Othello. What is the image that he has constructed for himself? How does society view him because of it? And what role does Othello's race have in his acceptance and rejection by characters in the play?

Today, students will close-read Othello's defense before the Venetian Court using the Choral Reading Essential. (We did some choral reading last week, but feel free to review more on choral reading in the Folger Method chapter.) This lesson supports students' active reading, speaking, and listening—and the speech makes clear Shakespeare's use of language and literary devices to develop our sense of Othello's character. It's a different way to take a deep dive into a text, providing them with strategies for reading and interpreting Shakespeare's texts as well as opportunities to see how volume, tone, or even physical distance between characters can shape an audience's experience of a scene. You provide and teach the strategies; students use them to take on significant analysis. And they will use these analytical tools far beyond Shakespeare.

Our students sometimes struggle when first reading verse; they treat one line as a whole idea, when the complete thought may run for more than one line of verse. Choral reading can be a useful exercise for helping students to "hear" complete thoughts in Shakespeare's verse. Since our focus today is on understanding Othello and his response to the events of 1.1, we've already divided the script for you. If you would like to create your own script or create an activity where students divide the script for themselves, the free, online Folger Shakespeare is your friend forever (shakespeare.folger.edu). It makes cutting and pasting the text of any play easy and convenient.

PS: If you're worried that your students will be turned off by so many readings of the same text, fear not and trust the process.

What Will I Need?

- Copies of Othello's defense (1.3.149–196, edited) – **RESOURCE #2.1A**

- Copies of the same speech, divided into two parts for choral reading for each student – **RESOURCE #2.1B**

- Paper or some device for written reflection

How Should I Prepare?

- Arrange the room so that ultimately you will have space to create two parallel lines of students in the center or at the front of the room.

Agenda (one 45-minute period)

❏ Part One—Quick Review: 5–10 minutes

❏ Part Two—Choral Reading: 15–20 minutes

❏ Part Three—Reflection/Discussion: 10–15 minutes

Here's What Students Hear (You Say) and (Then What They'll) Do

Quick Review:

1. Where are we in the plot?

[**TEACHER NOTE:** Wait for them to tell you.]

2. Revisit last week's reading: What did Iago, Rodrigo, and Brabantio say about Othello during the scene we read together?

[**TEACHER NOTE:** Ditto. Let them tell you and each other.]

Part One: Choral Reading

Here, we follow the steps for full Choral Reading, a Folger Essential.

1. **First read:** Using **RESOURCE #2.1A**, read the whole speech as loud and fast as you can while still staying together with the rest of the class.

2. **Second read:** Great job! Let's do that again, loud and fast. As you read it, think about how you feel when you must defend yourself. Try reading it that way.

3. By a show of fingers (1 = "I'm lost," 3 = "I've got this!"), indicate your understanding of the speech.

4. **Third read:** Okay, now let's read sequentially, person to person around the circle. Each person reads one line, then on to the next person.

   • As we read, mark any words or phrases you don't understand, and when we're finished reading, let's figure out what they mean together.

   • More thoughts on this speech?

5. **Fourth read:** Let's have two volunteers read the speech by alternating lines. One of you is Reader 1, the other Reader 2.

   • What more do you notice about this speech? What do you hear?

   • What do you think Othello is thinking about or feeling? How do you know? What does the text tell you?

6. By a show of fingers, indicate your understanding.

7. **Fifth read:** Now, try it in a different way, and switch to **RESOURCE #2.1B**. Let's form two equal lines that face each other. One line (half the class) is Side 1, and the other line is Side 2. Let's read the passage chorally, speaking the passage back and forth to each other.

   – What more did you notice about the speech in this reading? What lines or words helped you to develop these ideas?

8. **Sixth and seventh reads:** Read the speech a couple more times. Let's add volume and see what happens. Side 1, you shout your lines; side 2, you whisper. Then let's reverse who shouts and whispers and read again.

   – What did that feel like? Did one of those volumes feel appropriate, or more appropriate, for what Othello was saying and feeling? Why or why not?

9. After this reading, check again for understanding.

   – What new understanding do you have of the speech?

[**TEACHER NOTE:** If another reading is needed to boost comprehension, try one of these variations:

a. Start soft; each side gets increasingly louder.

b. Start loud; each side gets increasingly softer.

c. Each line takes one small step toward the center each time they read.

d. Lines begin facing each other and take one step away each time they read.

Follow this reading with a few more questions: What new understanding do you have of the speech? What was the effect of the new reading variation?]

Part Two: Discussion/Analysis

1. Now that you are well into this speech, what questions or observations do you have? Let's talk through yours first.

   I have some questions too:

   – How does Othello feel about having to defend himself? What does the text tell you?

   – How does Othello feel about Desdemona? How do you know?

   – How does Othello feel about himself? How do you know?

   – How would you describe Othello's personality, based on this speech? What does he seem to value in others? What does he seem to expect or demand of himself?

   – How does this differ from how Brabantio, Iago, and Roderigo in 1.1 feel about Othello?

Part Three: Written Reflection

Quick answers to these questions, please:

- How would you summarize this speech in one sentence?

- What do you think Othello will do or say next? What leads you to that prediction?

- If you were Othello, what would you do next?

[**TEACHER NOTE:** By the end of this lesson, students will probably have come to the realization that:

1. Othello and Brabantio were once friends.

2. Brabantio and Desdemona loved hearing Othello's stories about his past.

3. Desdemona and Othello fell in love.

4. Othello is one amazing storyteller!]

Here's What Just Happened in Class

- Students made sense of a complex speech by coming to it in several different ways—all collaborative and inclusive.

- Students explored multiple interpretations of words, lines, and meanings of Othello's defense speech.

- Students analyzed many aspects of the speech.

- Students predicted what Othello's next action could be.

- Students made a personal connection with Othello.

- Students did all of the above without you telling them anything. They're doing their own interrogation and analysis.

RESOURCE #2.1A

Othello 1.3.149–196 (edited)

OTHELLO

Her father loved me, oft invited me,
Still questioned me the story of my life
From year to year—the battles, sieges, fortunes
That I have passed.
I ran it through, even from my boyish days
To th' very moment that he bade me tell it,
Wherein I spoke of most disastrous chances:
Of moving accidents by flood and field,
Of hairbreadth 'scapes i' th' imminent deadly
    breach,
Of being taken by the insolent foe,
And being sold to slavery, of my redemption thence,
And of the cannibals that each other eat,
The Anthropophagi, and men whose heads
Do grow beneath their shoulders. These things to
    hear
Would Desdemona seriously incline.
She'd come again, and with a greedy ear
Devour up my discourse. Which I, observing,
Took once a pliant hour, and found good means
To draw from her a prayer of earnest heart
That I would all my pilgrimage dilate.
My story being done,
She gave me for my pains a world of sighs.
She swore, in faith, 'twas strange, 'twas passing
    strange
She wished she had not heard it, yet she wished
That heaven had made her such a man. She thanked
    me,
And bade me, if I had a friend that loved her,
I should but teach him how to tell my story,
And that would woo her. Upon this hint I spake.
She loved me for the dangers I had passed,
And I loved her that she did pity them.
This only is the witchcraft I have used.

RESOURCE #2.1B

Othello 1.3.149–196 (edited and divided)

SIDE 1: Her father loved me, oft invited me, / Still questioned me the story of my life

SIDE 2: From year to year—the battles, sieges, fortunes / That I have passed.

SIDE 1: I ran it through, even from my boyish days / To th' very moment that he bade me tell it, / Wherein I spoke of most disastrous chances:

SIDE 2: Of moving accidents by flood and field, / Of hairbreadth 'scapes i' th' imminent deadly breach,

SIDE 1: And of the cannibals that each other eat, / The Anthropophagi, and men whose heads / Do grow beneath their shoulders.

SIDE 2: These things to hear / Would Desdemona seriously incline.

SIDE 1: She'd come again, and with a greedy ear / Devour up my discourse

SIDE 2: My story being done, / She gave me for my pains a world of sighs.

SIDE 1: She swore, in faith, 'twas strange, 'twas passing strange,

SIDE 2: She wished she had not heard it, yet she wished / That heaven had made her such a man.

SIDE 1: She thanked me, And bade me, if I had a friend that loved her, I should but teach him how to tell my story,

SIDE 2: And that would woo her.

SIDE 1: Upon this hint I spake.

SIDE 2: She loved me for the dangers I had passed,

SIDE 1: And I loved her that she did pity them.
SIDE 2: This only is the witchcraft I have used.

"Put on your poker face, Brotha . . .": *American Moor* talks to *Othello*

Here's What We're Doing Today and Why

American Moor, Keith Hamilton Cobb's one-person 2019 off-Broadway play, uses the character Othello and the challenges of a Black actor auditioning for the part to explore the experiences of Black men in America. As a consideration of blackness as a construct in society, Hamilton's play works well with this week's focus on the place of Othello in the world of his play. Students have considered Othello as a character, but Hamilton explores Othello the man and the continuing intersectionality of race and privilege within Shakespeare's text.

Today, students will bridge the gap between art and life. As in *Othello*, Cobb's title character must defend his place in the world he has chosen. Students will be able to ground the character of Othello in a racial reality often overlooked by white actors playing a Black character. Students will explore passages from *American Moor* through the choral reading essential. In addition, students will see how Hamilton's text "talks" to *Othello* through a choral reading of what we call a SMASHED TEXT (a way to pair texts using two or more interwoven texts).

We end today with a written reflection that brings into focus the continuing issue of race in the play both for actors and for the character. Race and identity remain at the center of the study of *Othello* and while these discussions can be difficult, they are essential to our study of the play.

Agenda (one 45-minute period)

❏ Part One—Introduction: 5 minutes

❏ Part Two—Collaborative deep dive into *American Moor*: reading, cutting, presenting, discussing: 30 minutes

❏ Part Three—*American Moor/Othello* Smashed Text: 10 minutes

What Will I Need?

• Copies of a short excerpt from *American Moor*, one for each student – **RESOURCE #2.2A**

• Copies of the *American Moor/Othello* smashed text – **RESOURCE #2.2B**

How Should I Prepare?

• Figure out your groups of four, or decide if kids can group themselves.

• Read up on the Cutting the Text Essential in the Folger Method chapter.

Here's What Students Hear (From You) and (Then What They'll) Do

Part One: Introduction

Let's start off with some basic questions:

- Who gets to tell your story?

- How is a story influenced by the teller?

- What role does race play in our ability to tell our stories?

Part Two: Dig In—*American Moor*

We're going to spend some time with a play written in 2019 and performed all over the country and at the Globe in England. It's called *American Moor,* and it centers around a middle-aged African-American actor who is auditioning to play Othello in a production of the play directed by a young white director.

1. Okay, let's get into groups of four (no more than four). I'm going to give each group a piece of text from *American Moor* – **RESOURCE #2.2A**.

2. In your groups, work with your texts. You'll have 10 minutes to read it together in various ways so that you'll get to understanding.

3. Then your job is to cut that text in half. You'll have 10 more minutes to cut it down to what you see as the heart of the passage.

4. 20 minutes from now, each group will explain your process and your editing choices.

5. Let's hear your cuts and the reasons your groups made the choices they did.

[**TEACHER NOTE:** Students will disagree on what to cut, and this is evidence that they are analyzing, and grappling with meaning.]

Part Three: Smashed *Moor* and *Othello*

1. Let's look quickly at a smashup—**RESOURCE #2.2B**—and see where it takes us. Divide yourselves in half, and let's read it chorally, and twice so that everybody gets to read both parts.

2. Very quick conversation:
   - Initial observations or questions?
   - What is Othello feeling?
   - What is the Black actor, the American Moor, feeling?
   - What happens when we put the two together? Differences? Similarities?

Here's What Just Happened in Class

- Students brought together two different characters from two very different authors to illuminate elements of racial difference.

- Students collaborated with peers to critically read and edit a text and justified their editing choices.

- Students discovered that there is no single right interpretation of a text.

- Students used textual evidence to make inferences about characters and conflicts.

RESOURCE #2.2A

Excerpt from *American Moor*

The middle-aged Black actor is auditioning to play Othello. He's auditioning before the young white man who will direct the play. This is an imaginary conversation that the actor has with the director. And it begins with the actor referencing his audition to Othello's defense. Initial brackets added for clarity.

"... Put on your poker face, Brotha ..."
You think that he [Othello] thinks that he needs to do ... "a number" for these guys, in order to succeed in getting from them the thing that you think he wants ... And so, in order to get this gig, ah no wait! ... in order to succeed and getting from you the thing that you think I want ... you're implying that I need to do "a number" for you ...

It's brilliant. You're sitting there, looking expectantly at me, thinking we're speaking the same language. But you wouldn't understand a single word of all that's not being said ... if I said it ... if Othello said it ... I know that your intentions are good, young man, and that this is not your fault ... My anger, Othello's anger, the guard dog, forever snarling at his chain's end, sooner to strangle himself than acquiesce to your energy, he does not see you.

He sees all the hovering forces in this room, in that senate chamber, in the world that have made you you, as they are all the self-same forces that have never allowed me to be me. I'm sorry ... You stand in for so much, but I do too, and I cannot just be me, for you are never, ever, only you.

—from *American Moor*, p. 17
Keith Hamilton Cobb, 2020, *American Moor*, Methuen Drama, an imprint of Bloomsbury Publishing Plc

RESOURCE #2.2B

American Moor talks back to *Othello*

. . . Put on your poker face, Brotha . . .

Her father loved me, oft invited me,
Still questioned me the story of my life

You think that he thinks that he needs to do . . . "a number" for these guys, in order to succeed in getting from them the thing that you think he wants . . .

I ran it through, even from my boyish days
To th' very moment that he bade me tell it,
Wherein I spoke of most disastrous chances:

And so, in order to get this gig, ah no wait! . . . in order to succeed and getting from you the thing that you think I want . . . you're implying that I need to do "a number" for you . . .

Of being taken by the insolent foe
And sold to slavery, of my redemption thence,

It's brilliant. You're sitting there, looking expectantly at me, thinking we're speaking the same language.

It was my hint to speak—such was my process—

But you wouldn't understand a single word of all that's not being said . . . if I said it . . . if Othello said it . . .

She'd come again, and with a greedy ear
Devour up my discourse. Which I, observing,
Took once a pliant hour, and found good means
To draw from her a prayer of earnest heart
That I would all my pilgrimage dilate,

I know that your intentions are good, young man, and that this is not your fault . . . My anger, Othello's anger, the guard dog, forever snarling at his chain's end, sooner to strangle himself than acquiesce to your energy, he does not see you.

. . . in faith, 'twas strange, 'twas passing strange,
'Twas pitiful, 'twas wondrous pitiful.

He sees all the hovering forces in this room, in that senate chamber, in the world that have made you you, as they are all the self-same forces that have never allowed me to be me.

She wished she had not heard it, yet she wished
That heaven had made her such a man.

I'm sorry . . . You stand in for so much, but I do too, and I cannot just be me, for you are never, ever, only you.

She loved me for the dangers I had passed,
This only is the witchcraft I have used.

"Will Be Tenderly Led By The Nose": Exploring Iago's Plan through Soliloquies in 1.3 and 2.1

Here's What We're Doing and Why

Many of the different ideas about who Othello is—the "construct of Othello"—come from those who are already in Venetian society. Othello must figure out a way to both fit in and stand out. But there are large hurdles in his way; no hurdle is larger or harder than Othello's ancient—or ensign—Iago.

Today, we jump into the mind of "honest, honest" Iago by looking at the plan that he lays out in his soliloquies in 1.3 and 2.1. Students will already be familiar with the character of Iago and his "double knavery" thanks to their work earlier in Week One. Looking at the two soliloquies side by side, students will start to see the commonalities of language that Iago uses (bestial imagery) as well as his own racist biases (referring to Othello by name only once). Students will begin to discover a more complete understanding of the man at the very center of the tragedy.

Comparing the similarities and the differences in the speeches is another opportunity for students to practice their close-reading and character analysis skills. Establishing a firm foundation here at the beginning of the play will ensure that students can draw even richer conclusions about the character of Iago by the end of the play. Plus, Iago's willingness to manipulate the systems that are available to him underscores the precarious position in which Othello has unknowingly found himself. While it will just take the twisted mind of one man to bring "brave Othello" low, Iago's knowledge of how to achieve his aims demonstrates his privilege in his society and the upper hand that he holds over his general.

Agenda (one 45-minute period)

- ❑ Class Reading of 1.3.429–447 (Iago's "I Hate the Moor" speech): 10 minutes
- ❑ Class Reading of 2.1.308–334 (Iago's "That Cassio Loves Her" speech): 10 minutes
- ❑ Analysis, synthesis, and discussion of the two speeches: 15 minutes

What Will I Need?

- Copies of the two speeches, both in **RESOURCE #2.3**

How Should I Prepare?

- Make copies of **RESOURCE #2.3**.
- Decide how you'll divide the class into groups of four.
- Arrange your room so that all-class and group work is possible

Here's What Students Hear (From You) and (Then What They'll) Do

Part One/Warm-Up: Fast Choral Reading

1. Gather everyone in a circle, and let's read Iago's "I Hate the Moor" speech twice: once all the way through, and the second time to end punctuation.

2. What do you notice and understand about the speech? What is Iago thinking about? How do you know? What new info have you learned about him?

   – Is it clear what might be leading him to have these feelings? As we talk about them, who will write a list of Iago's *reasons* for hating Othello on the board or on chart paper?

3. Next, let's read Iago's second soliloquy twice in the same way. What do you notice and understand about the speech? And how do you know this? [**TEACHER NOTE:** Evidence from the text remains *always* important.]

   – What is Iago's plan? What details in the text lead you to know? Who will make note of Iago's plan on the board or chart paper so that we can reference it later?

   – Has Iago found clarity? How do you know?

4. As a rapid reaction to reading the two texts, what seems to be similar about Iago in the two speeches? Different?

Part Two: Synthesis and Analysis

1. In groups of four, read both speeches again, and then read them together. What are the similarities? What are the differences? In the language? In Iago's thinking? Take some time to discuss these questions and think them through.

[**TEACHER NOTE:** Circulate, don't participate, but see if students are noting similarities in the language, such as:

   a. Repetition of the word "ass"

   b. Reference to Othello by name (once) and "the Moor" (seven times)

   c. Repetition of "knavery"—what is knavery?

   d. "That thinks men honest that but seem to be so" vs. "he'll prove . . . a most dear husband."

   e. Who loves whom?]

2. Coming back together as a class,

   a. What do you notice when you compare these two speeches? What do you wonder? What other questions do you have?

   b. Your thoughts about Iago? A sympathetic character? Or not?

   c. Does the repetition of language between the two speeches reveal anything about him?

3. To conclude, write a reflection for the following prompt:

   a. Who is Iago? Answer this question in two sentences. Consider the language that he uses, the contradictions he seems to embody, and the power he has over characters in the play.

Here's What Just Happened in Class

- Students collaborated to analyze a key character in Shakespeare by close-reading and in-depth discussion of two of Iago's soliloquies from different parts of the play.

- Students learned that Iago's language gives him power.

- Students considered the larger issues of identity in the play by relating it to the villain Iago.

RESOURCE #2.3

"Excellent Iago, What's the Plan?"

1.3.429–447

IAGO
I hate the Moor,
And it is thought abroad that 'twixt my
  sheets   430
'Has done my office. I know not if 't
  be true,
But I, for mere suspicion in that kind,
Will do as if for surety. He holds me
  well.
The better shall my purpose work on
  him.
Cassio's a proper man. Let me see
  now: 435
To get his place and to plume up my
  will
In double knavery—How? how?—Let's
  see.
After some time, to abuse Othello's ear
That he is too familiar with his wife.
He hath a person and a smooth dispose
                                                   440
To be suspected, framed to make
  women false.
The Moor is of a free and open nature
That thinks men honest that but seem
to
  be so,
And will as tenderly be led by th' nose
As asses are.   445
I have 't. It is engendered. Hell and
  night
Must bring this monstrous birth to the
  world's light.
                                        He exits.

2.1.308–334

IAGO
That Cassio loves her, I do well believe 't.
That she loves him, 'tis apt and of great
  credit.
The Moor, howbeit that I endure him not,
                                                   310
Is of a constant, loving, noble nature,
And I dare think he'll prove to
  Desdemona
A most dear husband. Now, I do love her
  too,
Not out of absolute lust (though
  peradventure
I stand accountant for as great a sin)   315
But partly led to diet my revenge
For that I do suspect the lusty Moor
Hath leaped into my seat—the thought
  whereof
Doth, like a poisonous mineral, gnaw my
  inwards,
And nothing can or shall content my soul
                                                   320
Till I am evened with him, wife for wife,
Or, failing so, yet that I put the Moor
At least into a jealousy so strong
That judgment cannot cure. Which thing
  to do,
If this poor trash of Venice, whom I
  trace   325
For his quick hunting, stand the putting on,
I'll have our Michael Cassio on the hip,
Abuse him to the Moor in the rank garb
(For I fear Cassio with my nightcap too),
Make the Moor thank me, love me, and
  reward me   330
For making him egregiously an ass
And practicing upon his peace and quiet
Even to madness. 'Tis here, but yet
  confused.
Knavery's plain face is never seen till used.
                                        He exits.

"Reputation, reputation, reputation!": Cutting in *Othello* 2.3

Here's What We're Doing Today and Why

As Othello establishes himself as a positive presence, Iago must work harder and more fiercely to take the general apart. A lot happens in Act 2, scene 3. It is an alarming scene, as Iago works to get to Othello by manipulating Cassio and exploiting his alcoholism in order to ruin him. Remember that Iago feels Cassio was wrongly promoted, that Iago should have been promoted instead.

Today, students will make decisions about which parts of the text are most important to the play. Using the cutting-the-text essential, students will engage in a close-reading of the scene, eliminating whatever they deem unnecessary. They have already cut the Shakespeare play a bit, but the task today is a big one. Because there is *so much* happening in this scene, students might be reluctant to cut out anything. It is important to remind students that often when plays are staged (and especially Shakespeare plays), they are edited for any number of reasons, from time constraints to style choices to interpretation and preference. We are putting students in the driver's seat here along with directors, actors, scholars, and editors. They will determine the vital elements of the scene by arguing it out with each other about what stays and what goes. This is analysis, and this is all without your help.

By the end of class, students should understand that Iago's grand manipulation plan is working, Cassio gets drunk, Cassio and Montano fight, and Othello fires Cassio.

We end today with students who are on their way to performing their own interpretations of Act 2, scene 3 and have the confidence to approach any scene to come.

Agenda (one 45-minute period)

❏ Part One—Introduction: 5 minutes

❏ Part Two—Reading and Cutting 2.3, and Analysis: 40 minutes

What Will I Need?

- Print copies of 2.3.40–284 – **RESOURCE #2.4**

How Should I Prepare?

- Arrange your classroom into small groups for students (3 to 4 is ideal).

Here's What Students Hear (From You) and (Then What They'll) Do

Part One: Introduction: Two big thought questions and the task at hand

1. Big Question #1: What is a reputation?

2. Big Question #2: Why is your reputation important?

3. Task at hand: Today we are going to read a scene in which many reputations are on the line.

Part Two: Reading and Cutting 2.3, and Analysis

1. Divide yourselves into groups of four (no more than four), and for each of you here is a copy of **RESOURCE #2.4**, *Othello* 2.3.40–284.

2. This is a long and really important scene. You'll have 15 minutes to read it together chorally. Get busy!

3. After you've read it, each group will cut the scene in half—down to 120 lines. Work together and keep what you think is the most essential. You can cross out what to cut or highlight what to keep, but eliminate half the lines. You'll have 15 minutes to do your cutting. [**TEACHER NOTE:** Some students will ask you to define "line." Let them decide.]

4. Then each group will post your cut script and explain your cuts. They will probably differ from one another, so we'll all learn from each other. [**TEACHER NOTE:** Explaining the cuts is the most important part!]

5. As we wrap up, consider for a minute who you think is the most essential character in the scene and why. Share that with all of us as you leave class!

Here's What Just Happened in Class

- Students read and analyzed text.

- Students read and analyzed a pivotal scene in which Iago reveals himself.

- Students collaboratively evaluated the text and made decisions about the importance of characters and words.

- Students, working together, created meaning in their own groups and learned how other groups made theirs.

- You got out of the way!

RESOURCE #2.4

Othello 2.3.40–284

CASSIO I have drunk but one cup tonight, and that was   40
    craftily qualified too, and behold what innovation it
    makes here. I am unfortunate in the infirmity and
    dare not task my weakness with any more.

IAGO What, man! 'Tis a night of revels. The gallants
    desire it.   45

CASSIO Where are they?

IAGO Here at the door. I pray you, call them in.

CASSIO I'll do 't, but it dislikes me.   *He exits.*

IAGO
    If I can fasten but one cup upon him
    With that which he hath drunk tonight already,   50
    He'll be as full of quarrel and offense
    As my young mistress' dog. Now my sick fool
       Roderigo,
    Whom love hath turned almost the wrong side out,
    To Desdemona hath tonight caroused   55
    Potations pottle-deep; and he's to watch.
    Three else of Cyprus, noble swelling spirits
    That hold their honors in a wary distance,
    The very elements of this warlike isle,
    Have I tonight flustered with flowing cups;   60
    And they watch too. Now, 'mongst this flock of
      drunkards
    Am I to put our Cassio in some action
    That may offend the isle. But here they come.
    If consequence do but approve my dream,   65
    My boat sails freely both with wind and stream.

                Enter Cassio, Montano, and Gentlemen, followed
                by Servants with wine.

CASSIO 'Fore God, they have given me a rouse
    already.

MONTANO Good faith, a little one; not past a pint, as I
    am a soldier.   70

IAGO Some wine, ho!

   (Sings.) And let me the cannikin clink, clink,
   And let me the cannikin clink.
   A soldier's a man,
   O, man's life's but a span,   75
   Why, then, let a soldier drink.
   Some wine, boys!

CASSIO 'Fore God, an excellent song.

IAGO I learned it in England, where indeed they are
   most potent in potting. Your Dane, your German,   80
   and your swag-bellied Hollander—drink, ho!—are
   nothing to your English.

CASSIO Is your Englishman so exquisite in his
   drinking?

IAGO Why, he drinks you, with facility, your Dane   85
   dead drunk. He sweats not to overthrow your Almain.
   He gives your Hollander a vomit ere the next
   pottle can be filled.

CASSIO To the health of our general!

MONTANO I am for it, lieutenant, and I'll do you   90
   justice.

IAGO O sweet England!

   (Sings.) King Stephen was and-a worthy peer,
   His breeches cost him but a crown;
   He held them sixpence all too dear;   95
   With that he called the tailor lown.
   He was a wight of high renown,
   And thou art but of low degree;
   'Tis pride that pulls the country down,
   Then take thy auld cloak about thee.   100
   Some wine, ho!

CASSIO 'Fore God, this is a more exquisite song than
   the other!

IAGO Will you hear 't again?

CASSIO No, for I hold him to be unworthy of his place   105
   that does those things. Well, God's above all; and

there be souls must be saved, and there be souls
must not be saved.

IAGO It's true, good lieutenant.

CASSIO For mine own part—no offense to the General,   110
nor any man of quality—I hope to be saved.

IAGO And so do I too, lieutenant.

CASSIO Ay, but, by your leave, not before me. The
Lieutenant is to be saved before the Ancient. Let's
have no more of this. Let's to our affairs. God   115
forgive us our sins! Gentlemen, let's look to our
business. Do not think, gentlemen, I am drunk. This
is my ancient, this is my right hand, and this is my
left. I am not drunk now. I can stand well enough,
and I speak well enough.   120

GENTLEMEN Excellent well.

CASSIO Why, very well then. You must not think then
that I am drunk.
                                        He exits.

MONTANO
To th' platform, masters. Come, let's set the watch.
                                        Gentlemen exit.

IAGO, to Montano
You see this fellow that is gone before?   125
He's a soldier fit to stand by Caesar
And give direction; and do but see his vice.
'Tis to his virtue a just equinox,
The one as long as th' other. 'Tis pity of him.
I fear the trust Othello puts him in,   130
On some odd time of his infirmity,
Will shake this island.

MONTANO But is he often thus?

IAGO
'Tis evermore the prologue to his sleep.
He'll watch the horologe a double set   135
If drink rock not his cradle.

MONTANO It were well
  The General were put in mind of it.
  Perhaps he sees it not, or his good nature
  Prizes the virtue that appears in Cassio   140
  And looks not on his evils. Is not this true?
                                      Enter Roderigo.

IAGO, *aside to Roderigo* How now, Roderigo?
  I pray you, after the Lieutenant, go.
                                      Roderigo exits.

MONTANO
  And 'tis great pity that the noble Moor
  Should hazard such a place as his own second   145
  With one of an engraffed infirmity.
  It were an honest action to say so
  To the Moor.

IAGO Not I, for this fair island.
  I do love Cassio well and would do much   150
  To cure him of this evil—   *"Help, help!" within.*
  But hark! What noise?
                            Enter Cassio, pursuing Roderigo.

CASSIO Zounds, you rogue, you rascal!

MONTANO What's the matter, lieutenant?

CASSIO A knave teach me my duty? I'll beat the knave   155
  into a twiggen bottle.

RODERIGO Beat me?

CASSIO Dost thou prate, rogue?   *He hits Roderigo.*

MONTANO Nay, good lieutenant. I pray you, sir, hold
  your hand.   160

CASSIO Let me go, sir, or I'll knock you o'er the
  mazard.

MONTANO Come, come, you're drunk.

CASSIO Drunk?
                            They fight.

IAGO, *aside to Roderigo*

Away, I say! Go out and cry a mutiny. 165

Roderigo exits.

Nay, good lieutenant.—God's will, gentlemen!—
Help, ho! Lieutenant—sir—Montano—sir—
Help, masters!—Here's a goodly watch indeed!

A bell is rung.

Who's that which rings the bell? Diablo, ho!
The town will rise. God's will, lieutenant, hold! 170
You will be shamed forever.

Enter Othello and Attendants.

OTHELLO

What is the matter here?

MONTANO Zounds, I bleed
still.
I am hurt to th' death. He dies!

He attacks Cassio. 175

OTHELLO Hold, for your lives!

IAGO

Hold, ho! Lieutenant—sir—Montano—
gentlemen—
Have you forgot all sense of place and duty?
Hold! The General speaks to you. Hold, for shame! 180

OTHELLO

Why, how now, ho! From whence ariseth this?
Are we turned Turks, and to ourselves do that
Which heaven hath forbid the Ottomites?
For Christian shame, put by this barbarous brawl!
He that stirs next to carve for his own rage 185
Holds his soul light; he dies upon his motion.
Silence that dreadful bell. It frights the isle
From her propriety. What is the matter, masters?
Honest Iago, that looks dead with grieving,
Speak. Who began this? On thy love, I charge thee. 190

IAGO

I do not know. Friends all but now, even now,
In quarter and in terms like bride and groom
Divesting them for bed; and then but now,
As if some planet had unwitted men,
Swords out, and tilting one at other's breast, 195
In opposition bloody. I cannot speak

Any beginning to this peevish odds,
And would in action glorious I had lost
Those legs that brought me to a part of it!

OTHELLO

I pray you pardon me; I cannot speak.
How comes it, Michael, you are thus forgot?   200

CASSIO

I pray you pardon me; I cannot speak.

OTHELLO

Worthy Montano, you were wont be civil.
The gravity and stillness of your youth
The world hath noted. And your name is great
In mouths of wisest censure. What's the matter   205
That you unlace your reputation thus,
And spend your rich opinion for the name
Of a night-brawler? Give me answer to it.

MONTANO

Worthy Othello, I am hurt to danger.
Your officer Iago can inform you,   210
While I spare speech, which something now offends
me,
Of all that I do know; nor know I aught
By me that's said or done amiss this night,
Unless self-charity be sometimes a vice,   215
And to defend ourselves it be a sin
When violence assails us.

OTHELLO Now, by heaven,

My blood begins my safer guides to rule,
And passion, having my best judgment collied,   220
Assays to lead the way. Zounds, if I stir,
Or do but lift this arm, the best of you
Shall sink in my rebuke. Give me to know
How this foul rout began, who set it on;
And he that is approved in this offense,   225
Though he had twinned with me, both at a birth,
Shall lose me. What, in a town of war
Yet wild, the people's hearts brimful of fear,
To manage private and domestic quarrel,
In night, and on the court and guard of safety?   230
'Tis monstrous. Iago, who began 't?

MONTANO

 If partially affined, or leagued in office,
 Thou dost deliver more or less than truth,
 Thou art no soldier.

IAGO Touch me not so near.   235
 I had rather have this tongue cut from my mouth
 Than it should do offense to Michael Cassio.
 Yet I persuade myself, to speak the truth
 Shall nothing wrong him. Thus it is, general:
 Montano and myself being in speech,   240
 There comes a fellow crying out for help,
 And Cassio following him with determined sword
 To execute upon him. Sir, this gentleman
         (Pointing to Montano.)
 Steps in to Cassio and entreats his pause.
 Myself the crying fellow did pursue,   245
 Lest by his clamor—as it so fell out—
 The town might fall in fright. He, swift of foot,
 Outran my purpose, and I returned the rather
 For that I heard the clink and fall of swords
 And Cassio high in oath, which till tonight   250
 I ne'er might say before. When I came back—
 For this was brief—I found them close together
 At blow and thrust, even as again they were
 When you yourself did part them.
 More of this matter cannot I report.   255
 But men are men; the best sometimes forget.
 Though Cassio did some little wrong to him,
 As men in rage strike those that wish them best,
 Yet surely Cassio, I believe, received
 From him that fled some strange indignity   260
 Which patience could not pass.

OTHELLO I know, Iago,
 Thy honesty and love doth mince this matter,
 Making it light to Cassio.—Cassio, I love thee,
 But nevermore be officer of mine.   265
       Enter Desdemona attended.
 Look if my gentle love be not raised up!
 I'll make thee an example.

DESDEMONA

 What is the matter, dear?

OTHELLO All's well now,
 sweeting.   270

Come away to bed. *To Montano.* Sir, for your hurts,
Myself will be your surgeon.—Lead him off.
                              Montano is led off.
Iago, look with care about the town
And silence those whom this vile brawl
distracted.—   275
Come, Desdemona. 'Tis the soldier's life
To have their balmy slumbers waked with strife.
                              All but Iago and Cassio exit.

IAGO What, are you hurt, lieutenant?

CASSIO Ay, past all surgery.

IAGO Marry, God forbid!   280

CASSIO Reputation, reputation, reputation! O, I have
    lost my reputation! I have lost the immortal part of
    myself, and what remains is bestial. My reputation,
    Iago, my reputation!

"Speak. Who Began This?": Cut to Performance in *Othello* 2.3

Here's What We're Doing Today and Why

After their cutting work yesterday, students will work in the same groups to perform their scenes. This is another opportunity for students to put the text on its feet, this time with a script they have cut in the previous class. There is also a time limit today. Students will have the option to cut more of the scene if need be. But the overall goal for today is for students to refine their scripts and demonstrate that they can make changes and finalize decisions together. As we keep an eye on our end of the unit performance, today marks a key step toward the confidence and independence they will need during Week Five.

Agenda (one 45-minute period)

- ❏ Part One—Introduction/Cutting (more): 5 minutes
- ❏ Part Two—Create and Rehearse: 10 minutes
- ❏ Part Three—Performances: 25 minutes
- ❏ Part Four—Reflection: 5 minutes

What Will I Need?

- Student copies of *Othello* 2.3.40–284 from the previous lesson

How Should I Prepare?

- Arrange your classroom into small groups of students.

Here's What Students Hear (From You) and (Then What They'll) Do

Part One: Introduction

Everyone should have in hand scripts with the cuts you made yesterday. Refresh yourselves with these questions in your groups:

- So, what happened here in this scene?
- Who are the most important characters?
- What's a juicy line that you feel should not be cut?

Part Two: Create and Rehearse

1. Since you're expert editors by now, you will have 10 minutes to take your 120-line scene and turn it into a 5-minute version of this scene. And then you're going to perform your 5-minute scenes.

2. Feel free to cut more, but remember, do not compromise on meaning.

3. Decide who is going to play who, and map out entrances and exits.

4. Rehearse!

Part Three: Perform

1. Determine the order before you start.

2. Begin the performances!

3. As each group finishes, applaud wildly!

Part Four: Reflect

By way of reflecting, let's each of you give us one sentence that starts with the prompt. Let's go around the room, one at a time:

- I noticed . . .

- I resented . . .

- I wonder . . .

Here's What Just Happened in Class

- Students collaborated to further cut their scene and stage it.

- Students, in their performances, demonstrated an understanding of the characters, dialogue, and conflict.

- Students saw and demonstrated how easily a single lie can be the catalyst for catastrophe.

- Students got deep into the language, and therefore deep into Iago's orchestration and execution of a plot that reverberates throughout the rest of the play.

WEEK THREE: LESSON 1

"Peevish Jealousies": Tone, Emphasis, and Proximity

Here's What We're Doing Today and Why

Much of our work this week is focused on manipulation: its causes and effects in the play. Today, we will look at Iago's manipulation of Othello as he turns an innocuous conversation between Desdemona and Cassio into something much darker. Students will first look at proximity between actors onstage to consider how misunderstandings can be demonstrated before acting out this quick scene.

Students will then use tone and stress to consider how sentences can easily change their meaning based on our emphasis. Building off of the students' knowledge of Iago's manipulation of Cassio, they will see how just a slight shift in emphasis by Iago can bring into question what is expected of Othello by society in his relationship with his wife.

The last step today will be to put it all together: the proximity, tone, and stress before students end with a reflection about the manipulation that they have encountered today. Why do we allow simple misunderstandings and miscommunication to affect how we treat others? How could we rectify the situation? Exploring these ideas will allow students to tap into the larger questions of the play and to ask about whether the outcome was truly as "inevitable" as it seems.

Agenda (one 45-minute period):

- ❏ Part One—Group work on manipulation: 10 minutes
- ❏ Part Two—Read! Check for understanding! Analyze for tone and stress! Then perform!: 30 minutes
- ❏ Part Three—Debrief: 5 minutes

What Will I Need?

- *Othello* 3.3.1–44, edited – **RESOURCE #3.1**

How Should I Prepare?

- Read 3.3.1–44 on your own.
- Decide how you will divide the class into groups of four.

Here's What Students Will Hear (From You) and (Then What They'll) Do

Introduction

Today, we will look at the effects of manipulation on our characters. We start by looking at a conversation between Cassio, Desdemona, and Emilia and we'll see what Iago does with that conversation. We then look at how Iago uses language, including tone and stress, to manipulate Othello.

Part One: Group Work

1. Let's get into groups of four.

2. You will act out the following scenario with your group: Three friends are throwing a party and are talking about it when a fourth friend walks in on the conversation and mistakenly believes that he will not be invited to the party. Consider:

   a. *What* could the three friends say that might make the fourth friend feel this way?

   b. *How* could the three friends speak that might make the fourth friend feel this way (consider tone and stress)?

3. Give groups some time to practice before having a few groups perform for the class.

4. Now, return to your acting groups. Let's work with the same scenario, only this time, (1) no talking and (2) the fourth friend again mistakenly believes he will not be invited but he is standing on the other side of the room. Consider:

   a. What body language can be used to make the fourth friend feel this way?

5. Give groups some more time to practice before having a few different groups perform for the class.

6. When you bring the class back together, discuss:

   a. What did you do with your voices to make your fourth friend feel that he didn't belong?

   b. What did you do with your bodies to make your fourth friend feel that he didn't belong?

   c. Has this ever happened to you before? How did you deal with the situation? What advice would you give people who find themselves in a similar predicament?

Part Two: Read, Check, for Understanding, Analyze for Tone and Emphasis, and Perform!

1. Let's look at **RESOURCE #3.1**. Let's read the first part of the scene—ending with Desdemona's line, "Well, do your discretion." Read around the room, changing readers after each speaker.

2. Questions:

   a. What seems to be happening in this scene?

[**TEACHER NOTE:** Let your students tell you. They ought to be able to recognize that Cassio is still upset about his actions at the end of Act 2 and is trying to get Desdemona to plead on his behalf to Othello.]

    b. Which words or phrases are still difficult to understand, especially given what you already understand about the scene? Let's figure those out together.

    c. Anything else you notice about this scene? Anything particularly odd about the scene or the exchange?

3. Return to the script. Now read the rest of the scene, changing readers after each speaker. What do you notice about this side scene?

    a. Focus directly on the line "Ha, I like not that." Let's try reading this line, emphasizing a different word each time (**Ha**, I like not that; Ha, **I** like not that; Ha, I **like** not that; Ha, I like **not** that; Ha, I like not **that**.)

    b. What do you hear?

    c. What is Iago trying to achieve through this comment?

    d. Do you believe it can be/will be effective?

    e. What do you think Othello's reaction *should* be to this exchange? Do you believe that he will have this reaction? Why or why not?

4. Put this scene on its feet! Work in your groups and put the scene together quickly. Let's go back to the beginning of class:

    a. How might the group of three speak and act that might lead to misunderstanding?

    b. At what point in the conversation might Othello and Iago enter the scene? What would they see?

    c. How might Iago speak his line? Where should the emphasis be on his words?

5. When you've had some practice time, let's have a couple of groups show us their scene.

Part Three: Debrief

After the performances, ask students to consider in writing:

    a. What do you think leads to misunderstanding in group settings?

    b. How does proximity and/or tone contribute to misunderstanding?

    c. What do you think is the effect that this scene will have on Othello?

Here's What Just Happened in Class

- Students close-read Shakespeare's text in order to make an informed interpretive analysis of a scene.

- Students practiced using tone and stress to explore the subtext and meaning of a line.

- Students made connections between their lives and society and Shakespeare's text.

- Students learned how, even in Shakespeare, words can wound or warn.

RESOURCE #3.1

Othello 3.31–44, edited

Enter Desdemona, Cassio, and Emilia.

DESDEMONA

> Be thou assured, good Cassio, I will do
> All my abilities on thy behalf.

EMILIA

> Good madam, do. I warrant it grieves my husband
> As if the cause were his.

DESDEMONA

> O, that's an honest fellow! Do not doubt, Cassio,
> But I will have my lord and you again
> As friendly as you were.

CASSIO

> Bounteous madam,
> Whatever shall become of Michael Cassio,
> He's never anything but your true servant.

DESDEMONA

> I know 't. I thank you. You do love my lord;
> You have known him long; and be you well assured
> He shall in strangeness stand no farther off
> Than in a politic distance.

CASSIO

> Ay, but, lady,
> That policy may either last so long,
> Or feed upon such nice and waterish diet,
> Or breed itself so out of (circumstance,)
> That, I being absent and my place supplied,
> My general will forget my love and service.

DESDEMONA

> Do not doubt that. Before Emilia here,
> I give thee warrant of thy place. Assure thee,
> If I do vow a friendship, I'll perform it
> To the last article. My lord shall never rest:
> I'll watch him tame and talk him out of patience;
> His bed shall seem a school, his board a shrift;
> I'll intermingle everything he does

With Cassio's suit. Therefore be merry, Cassio,
For thy solicitor shall rather die
Than give thy cause away.

Enter Othello and Iago.

EMILIA

Madam, here comes my lord.

CASSIO

Madam, I'll take my leave.

DESDEMONA

Why, stay, and hear me speak.

CASSIO

Madam, not now. I am very ill at ease,
Unfit for mine own purposes.

DESDEMONA

Well, do your discretion.

Cassio exits.

IAGO

Ha, I like not that.

OTHELLO

What dost thou say?

IAGO

Nothing, my lord; or if—I know not what.

OTHELLO

Was not that Cassio parted from my wife?

IAGO

Cassio, my lord? No, sure, I cannot think it
That he would steal away so guiltylike,
Seeing your coming.

OTHELLO

I do believe 'twas he.

WEEK THREE: LESSON 2

"Why Did I Marry?":
Othello and Desdemona's Relationship (3.3)

Here's What We're Doing Today and Why

This week's work is all about manipulation—of language and actions—by Othello and, you guessed it, by Iago. We have not spoken directly about Othello and Desdemona's relationship outside of Othello's rebuttal in Act 1, but in Act 3.3 their relationship moves from the romantic ("for she had eyes, and chose me") to the repulsed ("O curse of marriage"). In the span of a single scene, Othello goes from deeply loving and being respectful of his wife to hating and demeaning her. What causes such an abrupt change?

Today, students will analyze the relationship of Othello and Desdemona. First by looking at their own approach to relationships and perhaps some traits that they might not even know they possess. Next, they'll examine their own biases as they relate to "cheating" and "jealousy" in a relationship based on their answers to some general, all-class questions, and, finally, they will have an opportunity to speak with each other about their understandings of how relationships work.

Students will then look at the beginning of 3.3 and work with staging to consider the current status of Othello and Desdemona's relationship at this point in the play. Students will move Othello and Desdemona between the AGREE and DISAGREE signs during Desdemona's pleas for Michael Cassio.

The last step will be for students to write a reflection on their feelings about Othello and Othello and Desdemona's relationship and how they see it pertaining to their own lives and the lives of their classmates. Asking students to consider how friends complicate their own relationships is worthy of reflection.

Agenda (one 45-minute period)

❏ Part One—Introduction and Decisions: 10 minutes

❏ Part Two—Read the Scene and Dig In: 20 minutes

❏ Part Three—Digging In Further: Showing Closeness Through Movement: 10 minutes

❏ Part Four—Written Reflection: 5 minutes

What Will I Need?

• Slides of your initial questions to project or distribute to the class

• AGREE and DISAGREE signs to hang in the classroom

• *Othello*, 3.3.45–102 – **RESOURCE #3.2**

How Should I Prepare?

- Read 3.3 on your own (it's very long!).

- Hang AGREE and DISAGREE signs on different sides of the classroom.

- Set up the classroom so that there is plenty of room for students to walk around.

Here's What Students Will Hear (From You) and (Then What They'll) Do

Part One: Introduction and Decisions

1. Today, we will look at the relationship between Othello and Desdemona. Please look back at your notes. What can you tell me about Othello and Desdemona and their relationship? [**TEACHER NOTE:** As always, let them tell you.]

2. Now let's have everybody stand in the middle of the room. You will be making decisions about whether you agree or disagree with the following statements. While you will get a chance to explain your decision, you cannot stand in the middle. You must make a choice to agree or disagree. I'll read the following questions aloud, each of you make your own decision about whether you agree or disagree, and move to the sign that reflects your decision:

   a. Flirting counts as cheating.

   b. Asking your partner for the password to their cell phone is healthy in a relationship.

   c. Your partner can be friends with people who have the same gender identity that they are attracted to.

   d. Your friends offer good advice about your relationship.

   e. Jealousy is healthy in a relationship.

3. Allow students to justify their choices through a general share-out after they have chosen sides.

4. Students can switch sides if they change their mind.

Part Two: Read the Scene and Dig In

1. Let's look at an interaction between Desdemona and Othello in **RESOURCE #3.2**. Read the script of 3.3.45–102. Read the scene around the room, changing readers after each speaker. [**TEACHER NOTE:** You may want them to read to end punctuation marks instead. You decide!] We'll read the scene twice if we need to.

2. After the class has read the scene, dig into questions:

   a. What is going on here? What does the text tell you?

[**TEACHER NOTE:** Students should get to the recognition that Desdemona is very interested in helping Michael Cassio and Othello eventually agrees. Let them get there themselves through discussion and analysis though.]

    b. Which words or phrases are still difficult to understand, especially given what you already understand about the scene? Let's hear them and let's figure out what they mean.

    c. Anything else you notice about this scene?

    d. How do you react to the scene?

    e. What is the current state of Othello and Desdemona's relationship? What makes you think so? What does the language tell us?

    f. Do you find anything worrying or troubling about the interaction?

Part Three: Digging In Further: Showing Closeness Through Movement

1. Let's have two volunteers stand in for Othello and Desdemona. The "actor" playing Othello will stand at the DISAGREE sign, while the actor playing Desdemona will stand at AGREE.

2. We'll all read the scene again, and this time in parts around the room.

3. After each speech, we'll ask if Othello should take a step toward Desdemona, indicating growing closer to her, or a step away from her, indicating more distance from her. This can be a small step or a LARGE step. Othello can move and Desdemona can move.

4. Now that we're finished, analysis questions:

    a. What questions do you have?

    b. What finally changes Othello's mind?

    c. How persuasive do you find Desdemona?

    d. What is the "witchcraft" that she has used?

Part Four: Written Reflection

Briefly jot down your thoughts on these questions at the end of class:

After this interaction, Iago tells Othello, "Look to your wife; observe her well with Cassio." Huh? Are there signs that there are problems in the relationship? Why would Othello need to "look to (his) wife"? What motive might Iago have for telling Othello to "observe her well with Cassio"? What role might jealousy play in the relationship? Does this relationship seem complicated at this point? Why or why not?

Here's What Just Happened in Class

- Students made connections between their lives and Shakespeare's text.

- Students close-read Shakespeare's text in order to make informed interpretive analysis of a scene.

- Students analyzed shifting character relationships through close-reading.

RESOURCE #3.2

Othello 3.3.45–102

DESDEMONA How now, my lord?   45
  I have been talking with a suitor here,
  A man that languishes in your displeasure.

OTHELLO Who is 't you mean?

DESDEMONA
  Why, your lieutenant, Cassio. Good my lord,
  If I have any grace or power to move you,   50
  His present reconciliation take;
  For if he be not one that truly loves you,
  That errs in ignorance and not in cunning,
  I have no judgment in an honest face.
  I prithee call him back.   55

OTHELLO Went he hence now?

DESDEMONA Yes, faith, so humbled
  That he hath left part of his grief with me
  To suffer with him. Good love, call him back.

OTHELLO
  Not now, sweet Desdemon. Some other time.   60

DESDEMONA
  But shall 't be shortly?

OTHELLO The sooner, sweet, for you.

DESDEMONA
  Shall 't be tonight at supper?

OTHELLO No, not tonight.

DESDEMONA Tomorrow dinner, then?   65

OTHELLO I shall not dine at home;
  I meet the captains at the citadel.

DESDEMONA
  Why then tomorrow night, or Tuesday morn,
  On Tuesday noon or night; on Wednesday morn.

I prithee name the time, but let it not   70
Exceed three days. In faith, he's penitent;
And yet his trespass, in our common reason—
Save that, they say, the wars must make example
Out of her best—is not almost a fault
T' incur a private check. When shall he come?   75
Tell me, Othello. I wonder in my soul
What you would ask me that I should deny,
Or stand so mamm'ring on? What? Michael Cassio,
That came a-wooing with you, and so many a time,
When I have spoke of you dispraisingly,   80
Hath ta'en your part—to have so much to do
To bring him in! By 'r Lady, I could do much—

OTHELLO

Prithee, no more. Let him come when he will;
I will deny thee nothing.

DESDEMONA Why, this is not a boon!   85
'Tis as I should entreat you wear your gloves,
Or feed on nourishing dishes, or keep you warm,
Or sue to you to do a peculiar profit
To your own person. Nay, when I have a suit
Wherein I mean to touch your love indeed,   90
It shall be full of poise and difficult weight,
And fearful to be granted.

OTHELLO I will deny thee nothing!
Whereon, I do beseech thee, grant me this,
To leave me but a little to myself.   95

DESDEMONA

Shall I deny you? No. Farewell, my lord.

OTHELLO

Farewell, my Desdemona. I'll come to thee straight.

DESDEMONA

Emilia, come.—Be as your fancies teach you.
Whate'er you be, I am obedient.
                    Desdemona and Emilia exit.

OTHELLO

Excellent wretch! Perdition catch my soul   100
But I do love thee! And when I love thee not,
Chaos is come again.   102

"There's Magic in the Web of It": What's Up with That Handkerchief?

Here's What Will Happen Today and Why

Today's jam-packed lesson explores Othello's famous handkerchief using performance and active close-reading to pose and answer the question: What exactly IS this handkerchief? And why is it so important? Throughout the work today, the handkerchief grows from a "napkin" that "falls, unnoticed" (3.3.331) to the "ocular proof" (3.3.412) that Othello needs to believe that Desdemona is indeed having an affair with Michael Cassio. It's a wild transition.

Students will dig into lines from 3.3 and 3.4 that portray the ever-increasing importance of the handkerchief. They will fill out a graphic organizer to see how their thinking about the handkerchief evolves over the course of the period and will have a bit of fun using tissues to add movement and emphasis to the scenes. By adding movement, tone, and stress, students will see how actions can help further the story that they are telling onstage.

The idea of Iago's manipulation of the handkerchief—from something small and seemingly innocent into something huge and visceral—mirrors his tactics throughout the play. Manipulation continues to play a large role in the plot of the play, but also in the development of the characters. How characters manipulate others and are themselves manipulated is at the crux of understanding the play. Today's work allows students to continue to see how this plays out.

What Will I Need?

- Copies of the Note Catcher for all – **RESOURCE #3.3A**
- Copies of the Handkerchief Scenes for all – **RESOURCE #3.3B, RESOURCE #3.3C, RESOURCE #3.3D, RESOURCE #3.3E**
- A box of tissues

How Should I Prepare?

- Read through the scenes. There is a lot that happens with the handkerchief here!
- Set up the classroom in a circle with a tissue on each chair.
- Make copies of the Note Catcher and edited scenes below.

Agenda (one 45-minute period)

- ❑ Part One: Intro and Pairs Read and Perform Othello and Desdemona in 3.3.321–333 – **RESOURCE #3.3B**

  Note-Catcher Reflection – **RESOURCE #3.3A** (13 minutes)

❏ Part Two: Active Group Read of Emilia and Iago and a Handkerchief in 3.3.334–343 and 3.3.344–359 – **RESOURCE #3.3C**

Note-Catcher Reflection – **RESOURCE #3.3A** (8 minutes)

❏ Part Three: Desdemona and Othello and a Handkerchief in 3.4.58-89 – **RESOURCE #3.3D** and in 3.4.103–115 (edited) – **RESOURCE #3.3E**

Note-Catcher Reflection – **RESOURCE #3.3A** (15 minutes)

❏ Part Four: Share-Out: What *IS* this handkerchief? (9 minutes)

Here's What Students Hear (From You) and (Then What They'll) Do

Part One: Intro and performance of 3.3.321–333

1. Today, we'll dig into the handkerchief scenes from 3.3 and 3.4 of *Othello*. By the end of class, you will be experts on this handkerchief! Everyone, please take a tissue and raise your handkerchief and wave it in the air:

   – Like you are trying to get someone's attention

   – Like you are flirting

   – Like you are angry

   – Like you are annoyed that a teacher is trying to make you wave a handkerchief in the air

   2. Now, choose a partner or work with the student to your right.

2. Here is the script for 3.3.321–333 – **RESOURCE #3.3B**. Get busy reading and figuring out how you will perform it.

3. Let's have a couple of groups perform, then how about these questions:

   a. Where are all the handkerchiefs? Why?

   b. What are your initial reactions to where the handkerchiefs are?

5. Quickly fill out the first column of your Note Catcher – **RESOURCE #3.3A**.

Part Two: Emilia and Iago and a Handkerchief

1. OK, now let's get on to the next scenes, and let's do that as a class in a big circle. Here's the script for 3.3.334–343 and 3.3.344–359 – **RESOURCE #3.3C**. As we read, stand and move however you'd like.

2. Read each section—in the first one, change speakers at every line. In the second, change speakers at each end punctuation mark. As you read, wave your handkerchiefs in the air each time the word "handkerchief" is said in the script.

3. Analysis:

   a. Where is the handkerchief now?

   b. Did you change how you waved the handkerchief depending upon who was speaking? What does this tell us about each character's motivation?

4. Quickly fill out the second and third columns of the Note Catcher.

Part Three: Desdemona and Othello and a Handkerchief

1. Next and almost last, here is the script for 3.4.58–89 – **RESOURCE #3.3D**.

2. Read each section, moving from speaker to speaker, changing at each punctuation mark. Again, wave your handkerchiefs in the air when the word is said in the script. As we read, move however you'd like.

3. Analysis: What is the story/mythology of the handkerchief? Does this fit with what we know about Othello as a storyteller?

4. Quickly fill out the fourth column of the Note Catcher.

5. Last . . . here is the script for 3.4.103–115 (edited) – **RESOURCE #3.3E**. And let me catch you up on a key development: Iago has told Othello that Cassio has the handkerchief. (Incredibly, this is not a lie . . . Iago planted the handkerchief in Cassio's room.)

6. Let's split the circle in two, with one half of you doing choral reading of Desdemona and the other half, choral reading of Othello. *DON'T FORGET TO WAVE THOSE HANDKERCHIEFS!*

7. Have groups read it a few different times, playing with their volume and intonation.

   a. What do you notice?

   b. What is the purpose of the repetition of the word "handkerchief," do you think?

   c. How do you explain Desdemona's actions in the scene?

8. Students fill out the final column of the Note Catcher.

9. Conclude class with individual share-outs around the circle: in one word, what IS the handkerchief?

Here's What Just Happened in Class

- Students collaborated to find movement in Shakespeare's text.

- Students used props and volume to play with a scene.

- Students interpreted a scene using evidence from the text.

- Students tracked the meaning of an important prop throughout multiple scenes and changing contexts.

- Students determined the significance of a key plot device.

RESOURCE #3.3A—NOTE CATCHER

"There's Magic in the Web of It": The Growing Importance of the Handkerchief

3.3.321–333	3.3.334–343	3.3.344–359	3.4.58–89	3.4.103–115
"Your napkin is too little . . ."	"Her first remembrance from the Moor . . ."	"It is a common thing . . ."	"Look to it well . . ."	"The handker-chief!"
I think . . .	I think . . .	I think . . .	I think . . .	I think . . .
I wonder . . .	I wonder . . .	I wonder . . .	I wonder . . .	I wonder . . .
I know . . .	I know . . .	I know . . .	I know . . .	I know . . .

Desdemona and Othello and a Handkerchief

Othello 3.3.321–333

DESDEMONA How now, my dear Othello?
    Your dinner, and the generous islanders
    By you invited, do attend your presence.

OTHELLO I am to blame.

DESDEMONA
    Why do you speak so faintly? Are you not well?   325

OTHELLO
    I have a pain upon my forehead, here.

DESDEMONA
    Faith, that's with watching. 'Twill away again.
    Let me but bind it hard; within this hour
    It will be well.

OTHELLO Your napkin is too little.   330
    Let it alone.   *The **handkerchief** falls, unnoticed.*
    Come, I'll go in with you.

DESDEMONA
    I am very sorry that you are not well.

RESOURCE #3.3C

Emilia and a Handkerchief

Othello 3.3.334–343

EMILIA, *picking up the **handkerchief***
    I am glad I have found this napkin.
    This was her first remembrance from the Moor.   335
    My wayward husband hath a hundred times
    Wooed me to steal it. But she so loves the token
    (For he conjured her she should ever keep it)
    That she reserves it evermore about her
    To kiss and talk to. I'll have the work ta'en out   340
    And give 't Iago. What he will do with it
    Heaven knows, not I.
    I nothing but to please his fantasy.

EMILIA AND IAGO AND A HANDKERCHIEF

Othello 3.3.344–359

IAGO How now? What do you here alone?

EMILIA
Do not you chide. I have a thing for you.   345

IAGO
You have a thing for me? It is a common thing—

EMILIA Ha?

IAGO To have a foolish wife.

EMILIA
O, is that all? What will you give me now
For that same **handkerchief**?   350

IAGO What **handkerchief**?

EMILIA What **handkerchief**?
Why, that the Moor first gave to Desdemona,
That which so often you did bid me steal.

IAGO Hast stol'n it from her?   355

EMILIA
No, faith, she let it drop by negligence,
And to th' advantage I, being here, took 't up.
Look, here 'tis.

IAGO A good wench! Give it me.

RESOURCE #3.3D

Desdemona and Othello and a Handkerchief

Othello 3.4.58–89

OTHELLO
I have a salt and sorry rheum offends me.
Lend me thy **handkerchief**.

DESDEMONA Here, my lord.   60

OTHELLO
That which I gave you.

DESDEMONA I have it not about me.

OTHELLO Not?

DESDEMONA No, faith, my lord.

OTHELLO That's a fault. That **handkerchief**   65
Did an Egyptian to my mother give.
She was a charmer, and could almost read
The thoughts of people. She told her, while she kept it,
'Twould make her amiable and subdue my father   70
Entirely to her love. But if she lost it,
Or made a gift of it, my father's eye
Should hold her loathèd, and his spirits should hunt
After new fancies. She, dying, gave it me,
And bid me, when my fate would have me wived,   75
To give it her. I did so; and take heed on 't,
Make it a darling like your precious eye.
To lose 't or give 't away were such perdition
As nothing else could match.

DESDEMONA Is 't possible?   80

OTHELLO
'Tis true. There's magic in the web of it.
A sybil that had numbered in the world
The sun to course two hundred compasses,
In her prophetic fury sewed the work.
The worms were hallowed that did breed the silk,   85

And it was dyed in mummy, which the skillful
Conserved of maidens' hearts.

DESDEMONA I' faith, is 't true?

OTHELLO
Most veritable. Therefore, look to 't well.

RESOURCE #3.3E

Desdemona and Othello and a Handkerchief

Othello 3.4.103–115 (edited)

OTHELLO
  Fetch me the **handkerchief**!

DESDEMONA Come, come.   105

OTHELLO
  The **handkerchief**!

DESDEMONA I pray, talk me of Cassio.

OTHELLO The **handkerchief**!

DESDEMONA A man that all his time   110
  Hath founded his good fortunes on your love;
  Shared dangers with you—

OTHELLO
  The **handkerchief**!

DESDEMONA I' faith, you are to blame.

OTHELLO Zounds!

WEEK THREE: LESSON 4

"By heaven, you do me wrong": Exploring Jealousy through Essentials Promptbooks

Here's What We're Doing Today and Why

Today is all about directing Shakespeare—putting the words in action—and over the next two lessons students will create directors' promptbooks. The promptbook is a Folger Essential because in creating one, a student pulls together the text with annotations that indicate line cuts, entrances and exits, stage movement, the set, props and costumes, and generally, within a certain production, how the scene should be performed. Students will create promptbooks for their final scenes; this one, around the relationship between Othello and Desdemona, is a great learning opportunity. In the world of theater, this has forever been, and still is, a common practice. Today we call them stage managers' books.

This excerpt from 4.2 will give students an opportunity to dig into the culmination of all of Iago's manipulations. And . . . all of you will have a chance to review images from a promptbook from an historic and groundbreaking production of *Othello* that took place in London in 1930. Paul Robeson played Othello to Dame Peggy Ashcroft's Desdemona—a historic production for two reasons:

- Paul Robeson was the first Black man to play Othello since Ira Aldridge did so in 1833. Before and after Aldridge (and long after Robeson too), Othello was only played by white men in blackface.

- Since Robeson was Black and Peggy Ashcroft was white, this mixed-race production took place in London because segregation made it impossible for it to take place in the United States. A decade or so later, though, in 1942, Paul Robeson and Uta Hagen (a white actress) appeared on Broadway in a wildly popular production of *Othello* that influenced American theater for years afterwards.

Paul Robeson (1898–1976) was a football All-American at Rutgers University. He played in the NFL while going to Columbia Law School. He became not only a lawyer but an accomplished and well-known actor and concert singer, known for his talent as well as his political activism.

What Will I Need?

- Two images from the Folger promptbook of Paul Robeson's *Othello* – **RESOURCE #3.4A** and **RESOURCE #3.4B**

- Copies of 4.2.37–105 – **RESOURCE #3.4C**

- Copies of Folger guidelines for creating a promptbook – **RESOURCE #3.4D**

- Pencils and erasers

How Should I Prepare?

- Make copies of materials.

- Review the 4.2 scene, the promptbook guidelines, and this lesson.

- Organize the class into groups of four and arrange your room to facilitate partner work (desks in pairs or spaces opened up for students to meet and work together).

Agenda (one 45-minute period)

❏ Introduction and a look at an historic promptbook from the Folger collection: 10 minutes

❏ Part One—Work through the Scene: 10 minutes

❏ Part Two—Create Your Promptbook: 20 minutes

❏ Part Three—Share on the Process: 5 minutes

Here's What Students Hear (From You) and (Then What They'll) Do

Introduction

1. First, let's look at these two images from a famous promptbook in the Folger collection. This promptbook memorializes what happened onstage during a groundbreaking production of *Othello* in London in 1930 – **RESOURCE #3.4A** and **RESOURCE #3.4B**. [**TEACHER NOTE:** Fill your students in on the context of this production, the importance of Robeson, all of that. All students should know this!]

2. What do you notice, and what do you wonder, about these pages? What was the stage manager marking down and making clear?

3. Today, we will create promptbooks focused on 4.2.37–105.

Part One: Work Through the Scene

1. Let's look at the scene – **RESOURCE #3.4C**.

2. Work in groups of four, and read the text aloud together.

3. Read the text aloud again.

4. Decide together what is happening in the scene and what the characters are feeling during the exchange.

5. In your groups:

    a. How would you summarize this scene in one sentence?

    b. How does Othello feel about Desdemona? How do you know?

    c. How do you think Desdemona feels?

    d. How does Othello's use of language change the way the audience may feel about his character?

    e. What else do you wonder about?

Part Two: Make Your Promptbook

1. As a group, take a look at the guidelines for creating a promptbook – **RESOURCE #3.4D** – and get busy.

2. Once you have all completed your promptbook, discuss together as a whole class:

    a. Which line was most difficult to assign an action to? Why?

    b. What is your most inventive direction? What led you to make it?

    c. What did you cut and why?

Part Three: Share on the Process

Rate your level of understanding of this scene on a scale of 1 to 10. What do you understand now that you didn't understand before? What do you think contributed to that understanding?

Here's What Just Happened in Class

- Students had a chance to examine facsimiles of rare materials.

- Students pulled together meaning, movement, vocal inflection, and more into a full treatment of the speech.

- Students made collaborative decisions about staging the play without your help.

- Students reflected on how their staging choices impact the audience's interpretation of the scene.

- Students applied their knowledge of character development and plot to interpret the scene.

- Students synthesized textual meaning into how a director might guide a performance.

- Students analyzed how previous directors have interpreted Shakespeare's text for staging.

RESOURCE #3.4A

Welcome to the Folger Vault!:

One of two pages from an historic *Othello* promptbook

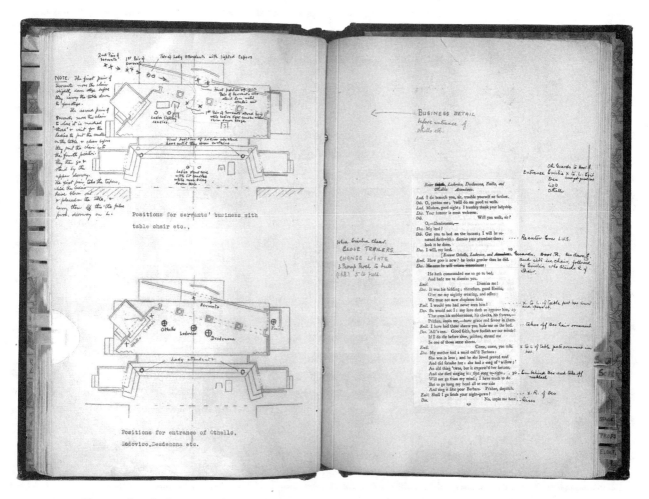

Promptbook for a production of *Othello* at the Savoy Theatre, London, with Paul Robeson as Othello, in 1930. Contains many ground plans and photographs of the set.

FROM THE COLLECTION OF THE FOLGER SHAKESPEARE LIBRARY, WASHINGTON, DC.

RESOURCE #3.4B

Welcome to the Folger Vault!:

Second page from an historic *Othello* promptbook

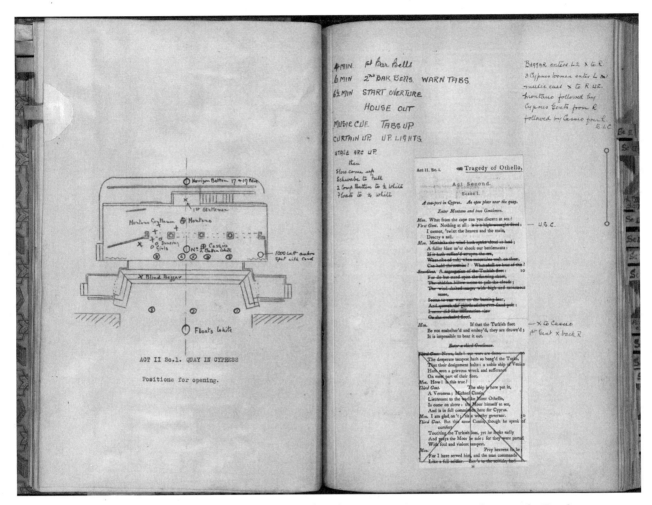

Promptbook for a production of *Othello* at the Savoy Theatre, London, with Paul Robeson as Othello, in 1930. Contains many ground plans and photographs of the set.

FROM THE COLLECTION OF THE FOLGER SHAKESPEARE LIBRARY, WASHINGTON, DC

RESOURCE #3.4C

Othello 4.2.37–105

DESDEMONA, *kneeling*
Upon my knees, what doth your speech import?
I understand a fury in your words,
But not the words.

OTHELLO Why? What art thou?   40

DESDEMONA
Your wife, my lord, your true and loyal wife.

OTHELLO Come, swear it. Damn thyself,
Lest, being like one of heaven, the devils themselves
Should fear to seize thee. Therefore be double
    damned.   45
Swear thou art honest.

DESDEMONA Heaven doth truly know it.

OTHELLO
Heaven truly knows that thou art false as hell.

DESDEMONA, *standing*
To whom, my lord? With whom? How am I false?

OTHELLO
Ah, Desdemon, away, away, away!   50

DESDEMONA
Alas the heavy day, why do you weep?
Am I the motive of these tears, my lord?
If haply you my father do suspect
An instrument of this your calling back,
Lay not your blame on me. If you have lost him,   55
I have lost him too.

OTHELLO Had it pleased heaven
To try me with affliction, had they rained
All kind of sores and shames on my bare head,
Steeped me in poverty to the very lips,   60
Given to captivity me and my utmost hopes,
I should have found in some place of my soul
A drop of patience. But alas, to make me

A fixèd figure for the time of scorn
To point his slow unmoving finger at—   65
Yet could I bear that too, well, very well.
But there where I have garnered up my heart,
Where either I must live or bear no life,
The fountain from the which my current runs
Or else dries up—to be discarded thence,   70
Or keep it as a cistern for foul toads
To knot and gender in—turn thy complexion there,
Patience, thou young and rose-lipped cherubin,
Ay, there look grim as hell.

DESDEMONA
  I hope my noble lord esteems me honest.   75

OTHELLO
  O, ay, as summer flies are in the shambles,
That quicken even with blowing! O thou weed,
Who art so lovely fair, and smell'st so sweet
That the sense aches at thee, would thou hadst
ne'er been born!   80

DESDEMONA
  Alas, what ignorant sin have I committed?

OTHELLO
  Was this fair paper, this most goodly book,
Made to write "whore" upon? What committed?
Committed? O thou public commoner,
I should make very forges of my cheeks   85
That would to cinders burn up modesty,
Did I but speak thy deeds. What committed?
Heaven stops the nose at it, and the moon winks;
The bawdy wind that kisses all it meets
Is hushed within the hollow mine of earth   90
And will not hear 't. What committed?
Impudent strumpet!

DESDEMONA   By heaven, you do me wrong!

OTHELLO   Are not you a strumpet?

DESDEMONA   No, as I am a Christian!   95
  If to preserve this vessel for my lord
From any other foul unlawful touch
Be not to be a strumpet, I am none.

OTHELLO What, not a whore?

DESDEMONA No, as I shall be saved.   100

OTHELLO Is 't possible?

DESDEMONA
  O, heaven forgive us!

OTHELLO I cry you mercy, then.
  I took you for that cunning whore of Venice
  That married with Othello.   105

Folger Guidelines for Creating a Promptbook

GROUP TASK:

Collaborate to make a promptbook with annotations that show how your group would stage the text. All your choices must be supported by your understanding of the text. Write clear, detailed notes in the margins (just like in the promptbooks you've seen) and on the text, marking specific words and lines. And just like the pages you've seen, indicate cuts too. Note those and your group decisions about the elements listed below.

1. **Mood / Tone**
   a. overall
   b. key moments
2. **Acting:** Describe what each character is doing.
   a. movement (gestures, exits, entrances, facial expressions)
   b. voice (tone of voice, stress, volume)
   c. emotion (nervous, angry, curious, elated, etc.)
   d. nonverbal human sound (laughter, sigh, cry, scream, etc.)
3. **Design:** as simple or involved as time allows
   a. set
   b. costumes and props
   c. lighting
   d. sound effects

Director's Vision: Include in your promptbook a few thoughts about the group's vision (interpretation) of the scene. Describe how your staging choices reflect the text.

   SHARE: Stay tuned until tomorrow's class!

"Alas, what ignorant sin have I committed?": Exploring Jealousy Through Your Promptbooks and 3D Lit

Here's What We're Doing Today and Why

In the previous lesson, students created promptbooks for an excerpt from *Othello* 4.2. Now it's time to put their versions of that scene on their feet. Through 3D Lit, another Folger Essential, students will see how the best laid plans of their promptbooks will translate to the stage. While the creation of the promptbooks allowed students to discuss and imagine how a play could be staged, this is a time for students to test those plans in action . . . to evaluate and revise their choices, watch other interpretations of the same scene, and discuss how different perspectives can change how a scene is staged.

In this quick version of 3D Lit, students will use the previous day's promptbook to guide their staging. Students should feel free to modify their promptbooks as they work. This is not at all about a product; rather, it engages all students in the process of learning about a scene and some of the many possible variations in this scene and all of Shakespeare. Your role as teacher is to facilitate the directors' work. Get out of the way as much as you can. You should not direct. This is the work of student directors because it continues to develop all students' skills and engage them in the work.

What Will I Need?

- Copies of Act 4, scene 2, 37–105 – **RESOURCE #3.4C** from the previous class, marked up promptbook-style.

How Should I Prepare?

- Arrange your room so they can go back into their original groups (desks in pairs or spaces opened up for students to meet and work together) and also perform for one another.

Agenda (one 45-minute period)

- ❑ Part One—Quick Review, Rehearsal, and Make Changes: 15 minutes
- ❑ Part Two—Perform your "improved" scene for the class: 20 minutes
- ❑ Part Three—Reflect: 10 minutes

Here's What Students Hear (From You) and (Then What They'll) Do

Begin to rehearse your scene as you have it in your promptbook, and make changes in your promptbook as you go. Then,

Part One: Quick Review, Rehearsal, and Make Changes

1. In their groups from yesterday, students practice scenes with two students as actors and two students as directors.

- Directors make decisions about the set and "build" the set with objects found in the classroom.
    - Are there any necessary props, furniture, or features?
    - Where are the entrances and exits?
- Directors place the actors in their positions for the start of the scene.
- Directors share what they noticed, what needs to change, and what might be missing.

2. Run the scene and make changes in your promptbook as you go. You'll have 10 minutes to run your scene and create a more complete promptbook.

Part Two: Performance

Let's perform our scenes for each other and celebrate the differences!

Part Three: Reflection

Close out the lesson with oral reflection rounds:

a. I noticed . . .

b. I learned . . .

c. I learned about myself . . .

Here's What Just Happened in Class

- Students pulled together meaning, movement, vocal inflection, and more into a full treatment of the scene.
- Students evaluated their own work and made revisions based on application.
- Students made collaborative decisions about staging the play without your help.
- Students reflected on how their staging choices impact the audience's interpretation of the scene.
- Students analyzed varying interpretations of the same scene.
- Students engaged with Shakespeare's language through performance.

"The Ills We Do, Their Ills Instruct Us So": Emilia and Lucille Clifton in Conversation

Here's What We're Doing Today and Why

Today, we will be opening up a conversation between the character of Emilia and the great American poet Lucille Clifton. Emilia has been a minor, though critical, character in *Othello* so far, and her role as Desdemona's foil—or opposite in some ways—increases as we get further into the play. Where Desdemona remains unaware of the world and of the growing problems in her relationship with Othello, Emilia is the realist, bringing harsh realities into her advice to Desdemona. Emilia comes across in her monologues as a very modern and informed woman, one who has seen her fair share of life and who can see through the manipulation that society and men try to force on women.

If they don't know her already, students can learn about Lucille Clifton (1936–2010), an award-winning African-American poet and writer. Lucille Clifton grew up in Buffalo, New York. She studied at Howard University, before transferring to SUNY Fredonia, near her hometown. She was discovered as a poet by Langston Hughes (via their mutual friend Ishmael Reed, who shared her poems), and Hughes published Clifton's poetry in his highly influential anthology, *The Poetry of the Negro* (1970). A prolific and widely respected poet, Lucille Clifton's work emphasizes endurance and strength through adversity, focusing particularly on African-American experience, family life, and women's survival skills in the face of ill health, family upheaval, and historic tragedy.

Students spent last week considering manipulations in the play, and will spend this week thinking about identity and image. We will read Emilia's (scathing) monologue from 4.3 and explore the connection it has to the present through a paired text reading of Lucille Clifton's poem "the lost women." By focusing on Emilia—her frankness and her truth—and by opening up a conversation between Emilia and Clifton, students can consider how society's adherence to gender roles has a negative overall effect in how women approach and see their world. Students will complete a mashup of the monologue and poem, bringing Emilia and Clifton in dialogue with each other.

Reflecting on the conversation between Emilia and Clifton, what questions do students see? Are there any solutions? Highlighting these texts together demonstrates that throughout history, there have been negative effects by the manipulation of not only individuals but of societal expectations at large. Whether it is an expectation about men's "honor" or women's subservience, the characters prove how detrimental and, in the case of the play, how disastrous these manipulations can be.

Agenda (one 45-minute period)

❑ Part One—Emilia's Monologue: 10 minutes

❑ Part Two—Clifton's Poem: 10 minutes

❏ Part Three—Mashups: 20 minutes

❏ Part Four—Quick Oral Reflection: 5 minutes

What Will I Need?

- Emilia's monologue 4.3.97–115 – **RESOURCE #4.1A**

- A copy of Lucille Clifton's "the lost women" – **RESOURCE #4.1B**

- Mashup of monologue and poem – **RESOURCE #4.1C**

How Should I Prepare?

- Make copies of the Emilia monologue and the Clifton poem.

Here's What Students Hear (From You) and (Then What They'll) Do

Part One: Emilia's Speech

1. Let's read Emilia's speech—4.3.97–115 – **RESOURCE #4.1A**—chorally, like we do.

   - Your thoughts about what seems to be happening in this speech?

   - What words or phrases are difficult to understand?

2. Let's count off by twos and read it differently, with group 1 and group 2 reading alternate lines.

   - Group 1 should read loudly, and group 2 should read softly.

   - What is the effect of reading the speech this way?

   - Have you understood anything more about the monologue?

3. Let's read it around to end punctuation. Can we have three to four volunteers do that?

   - Hear anything or learn anything by listening to it that way?

4. How does Emilia feel? How do you know? What larger ideas does Emilia touch upon in this speech?

   - Does it influence how you view her character? Last thoughts about this?

Part Two: Clifton's Poem

1. Let's read Lucille Clifton's poem "the lost women" chorally, together, as a class.

   What seems to be happening in the poem?

   - Are there any words that stand out or are difficult to understand?

2. As before, let's split into two groups, and read alternate lines.

   - Group 1 should read in a deep voice, and group 2 should read in a high voice.

3. What is the effect of reading the poem this way? Do you understand anything more about the poem?

4. Three volunteers to read to the question marks, please.

  – What is the speaker feeling?

  – What larger ideas does the poem touch on?

Part Three: Mashup

1. Now, gather into small groups to create a mashup of the monologue and the poem creating a single piece that has all of the lines from both texts [**TEACHER NOTE:** If they need an example, you can provide one – **RESOURCE #4.1C.**]

2. What might you need to think about as you create?

[**TEACHER NOTE:** You might bring these questions up if they don't . . . Where in the texts do the authors seem to be highlighting similar topics?

Are there any places where questions are asked? Are they answered in the other piece?

How can the mashup be read in a way that highlights the two voices, while also bringing unity to them?]

3. Let's hear all of your mash-ups!

Part Four: Quick Oral Reflection

• Let's go around the room. Each of you finish this sentence: When we put Emilia and Lucille in conversation with each other, I noticed:

Here's What Just Happened in Class

• Students brought together two different texts from two very different times to illuminate elements of identity—both in literary analysis and in their own lives.

• Students collaborated with peers to critically read and edit a text.

• Students used textual evidence to make inferences about characters and conflicts, and to reflect on their own.

• Students explored what they understand about the gender-based expectations in their own lives.

RESOURCE #4.1A

Othello 4.3.97–115

EMILIA But I do think it is their husbands' faults
    If wives do fall. Say that they slack their duties,
    And pour our treasures into foreign laps;
    Or else break out in peevish jealousies,
    Throwing restraint upon us.
    Or say they strike us,
    Or scant our former having in despite.
    Why, we have galls, and though we have some grace,
    Yet have we some revenge.
    Let husbands know
    Their wives have sense like them.
    They see, and smell,
    And have their palates both for sweet and sour,
    As husbands have.
    What is it that they do
    When they change us for others? Is it sport?
    I think it is. And doth affection breed it?
    I think it doth. Is 't frailty that thus errs? It is so too.
    And have not we affections,
    Desires for sport, and frailty, as men have?
    Then let them use us well.
    Else let them know,
    The ills we do, their ills instruct us so.

RESOURCE #4.1B

the lost women

i need to know their names
those women i would have walked with
jauntily the way men go in groups
swinging their arms, and the ones
those sweating women whom i would have joined
after a hard game to chew the fat
what would we have called each other laughing
joking into our beer? where are my gangs,
my teams, my mislaid sisters?
all the women who could have known me,
where in the world are their names?

RESOURCE #4.1C

Mashup Example

But I do think it is their husbands' faults
If wives do fall.
i need to know their names
those women i would have walked with
Say that they slack their duties,
And pour our treasures into foreign laps;
Or else break out in peevish jealousies,
Throwing restraint upon us.
Or say they strike us,
Or scant our former having in despite.
jauntily the way men go in groups
swinging their arms
Why, we have galls, and though we have some grace,
Yet have we some revenge.
and the ones
Let husbands know
Their wives have sense like them.
those sweating women whom i would have joined
after a hard game to chew the fat
They see, and smell,
And have their palates both for sweet and sour,
As husbands have.
what would we have called each other laughing
joking into our beer?
What is it that they do
When they change us for others? Is it sport?
I think it is. And doth affection breed it?
I think it doth. Is 't frailty that thus errs? It is so too.
where are my gangs,
my teams, my mislaid sisters?
And have not we affections,
Desires for sport, and frailty, as men have?
all the women who could have known me,
Then let them use us well.
Else let them know
where in the world are their names?
The ills we do, their ills instruct us so.

"O, I Am Spoiled, Undone by Villains": Identity and Image

Here's What We're Doing Today and Why

Week Four brings with it the end of the play and, yes, the murder of Desdemona. We are about to see the character Othello do something unspeakable. This lesson works to bring together our earlier work on identity in order to create a deeper understanding of who Othello was, is, and will be going forward in Act 5.

We will ask students to participate in a gallery walk focused on the paintings of Kehinde Wiley and images from the Folger collection depicting various ways that Othello has been played. Wiley is an American painter who is known for his portraits blending modern subjects with classical themes. In 2017, Wiley was commissioned to paint a portrait of President Barack Obama for the Smithsonian National Portrait Gallery. Wiley's paintings explore identity through a lens of strength and honor reminiscent of the way that Othello unfolds the story of his life.

We will then compare and contrast Wiley's modern work with images that show us ways in which Othello has been portrayed on the stage and in the public consciousness. Students will reflect and discuss, in small groups and as a class, the power of image and the role that it has in our perception of others. Students will question the role that agency plays in our understanding of others.

What Will I Need?

- Images of five paintings by Kehinde Wiley – **RESOURCES #4.2A through #4.2E**

- Image of Ira Aldridge as Othello – **RESOURCE #4.2F**

- Images of other actors playing Othello from the Folger Collection – **RESOURCES #4.2G through #4.2K**

How Should I Prepare?

- Hang Kehinde Wiley's paintings around the classroom.

- Arrange the room so that students can move freely from picture to picture.

Agenda (one 45-minute period)

- ❏ Quick Review: 5 minutes

- ❏ Gallery Walk: 10 minutes

- ❏ Image Response and Analysis—Ira Aldridge: 5 minutes

- ❏ Image Response and Analysis—Othello: 10 minutes

❏ Small Group Discussion: 5 minutes

❏ Whole-Group Reflection/Analysis: 10 minutes

Here's What Students Hear (You Say) and (Then What They'll) Do

Quick Review:

1. Where are we in the plot? Revisit our work so far: Who is Othello at this point in the play? [**TEACHER NOTE:** Let them tell you and each other.]

Part One: Gallery Walk of Kehinde Wiley's Paintings

1. You'll see that there are images of paintings around the room for you to take in. These are paintings by an important living artist named Kehinde Wiley. And I'll tell you a bit about him.

   Walk around the room, look at each one, and take notes on each. You'll have roughly 2 minutes at each painting. Think about these things:
   - What interests you about this painting?
   - How does the painter feel about his subject?
   - Why do you think the painter presents his subjects this way?

2. Let's share out what you've observed. [**TEACHER NOTE:** Follow-up questions might include: What is the feeling that Wiley has about his subjects? Consider his use of color, scale, and framing.]

3. Do Wiley's paintings change *your* feelings toward his subjects? How? Why?

Part Two: Image Response—Ira Aldridge

1. We're now going to look at images of Othello from the Folger collection. Remind students that while Shakespeare clearly establishes Othello as a Black man, Othello was played by a white man in blackface—for 220 years of performances. It was not until Ira Aldridge played Othello, initially in 1825 and then in 1833, that the role was performed by a Black actor.

2. First, we'll look at this image of Ira Aldridge from the Folger collection – **RESOURCE #4.2F**. In writing, quickly answer:
   - What might it mean for the character of Othello that he was portrayed this way onstage?
   - What feelings do the images of Ira Aldrige elicit?
   - How do they make you feel about the character of Othello?

[**TEACHER NOTE:** As they reflect, hang up or project the historic images of actors playing Othello elsewhere in the room.]

Part Three: Image Response—Othello

Now we'll respond to a series of other historic images from the Folger collection –

RESOURCES #4.2G through #4.2K. These are actors playing Othello. In writing, record your initial observations. These prompts might be helpful:

- What do you see?

- What stands out about the image?

- What do you think is missing from the image?

- What is the overall effect of the image?

Part Four: Small Group Discussion

Next, let's move into groups of four to consider all of the images you have just seen. You may want to think about:

- What image stood out to you the most? Why?

- What are some big differences between the images? Explain.

- Why might there be these differences?

- What differences do you see between the paintings of Kehinde Wiley and the portrayal of Othello in these images?

Let's share your experiences of these images among groups.

Part Five: Whole-Group Reflection/Analysis

Othello began the play as "valiant Othello" and by now, at the end of Act 4, his status as the "noble Moor" is in question. In light of the images that you have just seen:

- Why does representation matter?

- How does your image tell your story?

- Why does it matter who tells your story?

- Who is more important, the image bearer or the image maker?

Here's What Just Happened in Class

- Students explored the complexities of identity through a gallery walk featuring a broad range of images.

- Students considered the role that representation plays in our understanding of character.

- Students analyzed historical representations of racialized characters.

- Students analyzed a character's transformation throughout the play.

- Students synthesized knowledge about a character through their textual analysis in conversation with artistic representations.

RESOURCE #4.2A

Napoleon Leading the Army over the Alps by Kehinde Wiley, part of his
Rumors of War series depicting military men on horseback.
2005, BROOKLYN MUSEUM, NEW YORK.

RESOURCE #4.2B

Passing/Posing (Assumption) by Kehinde Wiley.
2003, BROOKLYN MUSEUM, NEW YORK.

RESOURCE #4.2C

Miss Susanna Gale by Kehinde Wiley, After Sir Joshua Reynolds.
2009, BROOKLYN MUSEUM, NEW YORK.

RESOURCE #4.2D

Passing/Posing (Female Prophet Deborah) by Kehinde Wiley.
2003, BROOKLYN MUSEUM, NEW YORK.

RESOURCE #4.2E

Passing/Posing (Immaculate Consumption) by Kehinde Wiley.
2003, BROOKLYN MUSEUM, NEW YORK.

RESOURCE #4.2F

An advertisement for Ira Aldridge's performance as Othello at the Théâtre Royal Saint-Hubert in Brussels on July 19, 1852, the first performance of his European tour

FROM THE COLLECTION OF THE FOLGER SHAKESPEARE LIBRARY, WASHINGTON, DC.

RESOURCE #4.2G

Image of Mr. Grist as Othello, late 19th century

FROM THE COLLECTION OF THE FOLGER SHAKESPEARE LIBRARY, WASHINGTON, DC.

RESOURCE #4.2H

Image of John Tenniel as Othello, 1876

RESOURCE #4.21

Image of G.V. Brooke as Othello, between 1850 and 1876, London

RESOURCE #4.2J

An engraving of Mr. G.V. Brooke by Thomas Hollis based on a daguerreotype by
Fitzgibbon, mid-19th century, London

FROM THE COLLECTION OF THE FOLGER SHAKESPEARE LIBRARY, WASHINGTON, DC.

RESOURCE #4.2K

Walter Hampden as Othello

Image of Walter Hampden as Othello by Bert Sharkey, early 20th century, New York
FROM THE COLLECTION OF THE FOLGER SHAKESPEARE LIBRARY, WASHINGTON, DC.

WEEK FOUR: LESSON 3

"And Smote Him, Thus": A 20-Minute Act 5

Here's What We're Doing Today and Why

Students will produce their own 20-minute version of *Othello*, Act 5. This Folger Essential is an express tour through the play's toughest scene, and will give students an opportunity to engage with the plot through the language and set all of you up for the discussions and analysis for the rest of the week. As students are headed toward putting together performances of scenes from the play next week, this is an activity that will get them moving and speaking.

Today's lesson builds on the work of identity from the day before. Othello is almost unrecognizable as a character when he enters in Act 5—he is a man at his breaking point, ready to kill his wife. But by the end, he has tried to redeem himself once again through story. Students should continue to consider the image put forth by the play about our protagonist and if he can, or ever should, be redeemed.

Agenda (one 45-minute period)

❑ Producing and performing your 20-minute Act 5: 20 minutes

❑ Rapid-fire Reflection: 10 minutes

❑ Making broader connections: 15 minutes

What Will I Need?

- Single lines from Othello – **RESOURCE #4.3A**

- 20-minute *Othello* narration – **RESOURCE #4.3B**

How Should I Prepare?

- Print the single lines from *Othello* Act 5, ready to hand to students.

- Print the narration for you to read.

Here's What Students Hear (From You) and (Then What They'll) Do

Part One: 20-minute Act 5

1. I'm going to hand you a sheet with 24 lines from Act 5 (**RESOURCE #4.3A**). [**TEACHER NOTE:** You can also project these.]

2. Let's go around the circle as each of you read one line, then on to the next.

3. Now let's partner up in pairs. You own whatever line(s) you just read. Take a

few minutes to read over the lines that you both have, then come up with an action for each of the lines.

4. So now, let's put together your Act 5. I'll read the story, and as I do, I'll call out the number of the line that comes next (**RESOURCE #4.3B**). When your line comes up, pairs come into the circle and perform them.

5. Wild applause!

Part Two: Rapid-fire Reflection Rounds

Stay in your big circle. Respond to the following prompts with a word or one short sentence. We'll go around the circle so everyone can answer.

a. I noticed . . .

b. I wondered . . .

c. I struggled with . . .

d. I was frustrated by . . .

Part Three: Making Broader Connections

Let's look at some of these lines more closely.

- Are there lines that seem problematic?
- Let's read through them together.
- What do you notice about these lines?
- How do they affect the way you see Othello as a character?
- What about other characters?
- How do they affect the way you see *Othello* as a play?

Exit Ticket:

Choose a character from this scene and write one or two sentences from their perspective on why they made the choices they did during this scene.

Here's What Just Happened in Class

- Students collaborated with one another and got familiar with key lines and the plot of *Othello* Act 5.
- Students' voices were amplified and they made decisions about how to interpret the text through movement.
- Students made connections to how characters developed and changed throughout the course of the play.
- Students used textual evidence to analyze characters' perspectives and how they influenced their actions.
- You got out of the way and allowed students to do all of this on their own.

RESOURCE #4.3A

Lines for 20-minute Act 5

1. AY, LET HER ROT AND PERISH AND BE DAMNED TONIGHT, FOR SHE SHALL NOT LIVE. NO, MY HEART HAS TURNED TO STONE.

2. STRANGLE HER IN HER BED.

3. GOOD, GOOD. THE JUSTICE OF IT PLEASES.

4. AND FOR CASSIO, LET ME BE HIS UNDERTAKER.

5. HERE, AT THY HAND. BE BOLD AND TAKE THY STAND.

6. VILLAIN, THOU DIEST!

7. O, I AM SLAIN!

8. I AM MAIMED FOREVER

9. O, HELP HO! LIGHT! A SURGEON!

10. I AM SPOILED, UNDONE BY VILLAINS!

11. O HELP ME HERE!

12. O DAMNED IAGO. O INHUMAN DOG

13. O BRAVE IAGO, HONEST AND JUST

14. ONE MORE AND THIS THE LAST

15. WHY I SHOULD FEAR I KNOW NOT . . . BUT YET I FEEL FEAR.

16. THAT HANDKERCHIEF THAT I SO LOVED AND GAVE THEE, THOU GAV'ST TO CASSIO

17. I NEVER DID OFFEND YOU IN MY LIFE . . . NEVER LOVED CASSIO

18. KILL ME TOMORROW, LET ME LIVE TONIGHT

19. O FALSELY FALSELY MURDERS

20. NOBODY. I MYSELF. FAREWELL. COMMEND ME TO MY LORD.

21. FOR THOU HAST KILLED THE SWEETEST INNOCENT THAT E'ER DID LIFT UP EYE.

22. DEMAND ME NOTHING. WHAT YOU KNOW, YOU KNOW. FROM THIS TIME FORTH I NEVER WILL SPEAK WORD.

23. SOFT YOU. A WORD OR TWO BEFORE YOU GO.

    I HAVE DONE THE STATE SOME SERVICE, AND THEY KNOW 'T.

    NO MORE OF THAT. I PRAY YOU IN YOUR LETTERS,

    WHEN YOU SHALL THESE UNLUCKY DEEDS RELATE,

SPEAK OF ME AS I AM. NOTHING EXTENUATE,

NOR SET DOWN AUGHT IN MALICE. THEN MUST YOU SPEAK

OF ONE THAT LOVED NOT WISELY, BUT TOO WELL;

OF ONE NOT EASILY JEALOUS, BUT BEING WROUGHT,

PERPLEXED IN THE EXTREME . . .

24. THIS HEAVY ACT WITH HEAVY HEART

RESOURCE #4.3B

A Snapshot of *Othello* Act 5—Narrative

Othello believes everything that Iago has told him. Othello says: [**1. AY, LET HER ROT AND PERISH AND BE DAMNED TONIGHT, FOR SHE SHALL NOT LIVE. NO, MY HEART HAS TURNED TO STONE.**] Iago suggests: [**2. STRANGLE HER IN HER BED.**] and Othello agrees: [**3. GOOD, GOOD. THE JUSTICE OF IT PLEASES.**]

But there is more! Iago agrees that he will kill Cassio [**4. AND FOR CASSIO, LET ME BE HIS UNDERTAKER.**], but on the night of the murder, he convinces Roderigo to do it instead [**5. HERE, AT THY HAND. BE BOLD AND TAKE THY STAND.**]. And while Roderigo tries [**6. VILLAIN, THOU DIEST**], Cassio stabs him, killing Roderigo who says: [**7. O, I AM SLAIN!**].

Cassio doesn't leave unscathed [**8. I AM MAIMED FOREVER**], as Iago finally takes matters into his own hands and stabs Cassio in the leg [**9. O, HELP HO! LIGHT! A SURGEON!**]. When it becomes clear that Cassio is not going to die though he says: [**10. I AM SPOILED, UNDONE BY VILLAINS**], Iago reverses course and finds the not-quite-dead body of Roderigo [**11. O HELP ME HERE!**] and stabs him. Roderigo's last words: [**12. O DAMNED IAGO. O INHUMAN DOG**].

The voice of Cassio, yelling in the street, signals to Othello that Iago has kept up his part of the plan [**13. O BRAVE IAGO, HONEST AND JUST**] and Othello heads into Desdemona's bedchamber to kill her. As he builds up the courage to murder her, Othello kisses sleeping Desdemona [**14. ONE MORE AND THIS THE LAST**] and wakes her up. She says: [**15. WHY I SHOULD FEAR I KNOW NOT . . . BUT YET I FEEL FEAR**].

Othello accuses Desdemona of loving Cassio [**16. THAT HANDKERCHIEF THAT I SO LOVED AND GAVE THEE, THOU GAV'ST TO CASSIO**], but Desdemona proclaims her innocence [**17. I NEVER DID OFFEND YOU IN MY LIFE . . . NEVER LOVED CASSIO**]. Although she begs Othello to reconsider [**18. KILL ME TOMORROW, LET ME LIVE TONIGHT**], Othello will not be swayed.

And he smothers her.

Immediately, Emilia is pounding at the door, begging to be let in and inform Othello of the killings [**19. O FALSELY FALSELY MURDERS**], only to find Desdemona on her last breath, unwilling to name her murderer. She says: [**20. NOBODY. I MYSELF. FAREWELL. COMMEND ME TO MY LORD.**] Emilia is incensed and screams at Othello [**21. FOR THOU HAST KILLED THE SWEETEST INNOCENT THAT E'ER DID LIFT UP EYE**].

Emilia's screaming brings Gratiano, Ludovico, and Iago into the bedchamber. Emilia reveals the whole plot just before Iago stabs her. When asked for his reasons, Iago replies [**22. DEMAND ME NOTHING. WHAT YOU KNOW, YOU KNOW. FROM THIS TIME FORTH I NEVER WILL SPEAK WORD**].

And he doesn't.

As the full weight of his actions hits Othello, he decides to take his own life. Before he does so, he tells us how to speak of him:

[**23. SOFT YOU. A WORD OR TWO BEFORE YOU GO.**

I HAVE DONE THE STATE SOME SERVICE, AND THEY KNOW 'T.
NO MORE OF THAT. I PRAY YOU IN YOUR LETTERS,
WHEN YOU SHALL THESE UNLUCKY DEEDS RELATE,
SPEAK OF ME AS I AM. NOTHING EXTENUATE,
NOR SET DOWN AUGHT IN MALICE. THEN MUST YOU SPEAK
OF ONE THAT LOVED NOT WISELY, BUT TOO WELL;
OF ONE NOT EASILY JEALOUS, BUT BEING WROUGHT,
PERPLEXED IN THE EXTREME . . .]
And that is how it is told [**24. THIS HEAVY ACT WITH HEAVY HEART**].

"To Die Upon a Kiss": Determining Identity Through Othello's Final Monologues

Here's What We're Doing Today and Why

In 5.2, Othello delivers three harrowing monologues that chart his emotional journey in the scene—from rage, to remorse, to resignation. Othello the storyteller goes back to the well to try to shape the narrative of his life one final time.

Today, students will read Othello's monologues from 5.2 and compare them to see how much Othello has changed over the course of the play. Students will consider how Othello's words shape how we receive him and how his words affect the image of him that we are left with as the play closes. Students will cut these monologues, boiling them down to their five most important lines. Students will then use these lines as captions for their own images and work to defend these choices through reflection.

What Will I Need?

- Printed or projected image of Othello from Folger collection – **RESOURCE #4.4A**

- Copies of Othello's 5.2 monologues – **RESOURCE #4.4B**

How Should I Prepare?

- Make copies of materials.

- Organize the class into groups of four and arrange your room for group work.

Agenda (one 45-minute period)

- ❏ Warm-up: 5 minutes

- ❏ Othello's 5.2 monologues: 10 minutes

- ❏ Speech cutting: 10 minutes

- ❏ Image captioning: 15 minutes

- ❏ Writing: 5 minutes

What Students Hear (From You) and (Then What They'll) Do

Warm-up

Let's look at this image from the Folger collection – **RESOURCE #4.4A**.

- What do you notice about this image? What do you wonder?

- Based on this image, how are we supposed to feel about Othello? How do you know?

Part One: Speech Study

1. Let's get into groups of four and take a look at the three monologues that Othello has in Act 5 – **RESOURCE #4.4B**.

2. In your groups, read each of Othello's monologues, changing readers at end punctuation marks. After each monologue, start your analysis:

   a. What do you notice? What do you wonder?

   b. What conflicts do you hear in Othello's monologues? Are these internal or external conflicts?

   c. What decision or realization does Othello reach by the end of each monologue?

   d. How do you react personally to these decisions and realizations?

Part Two: Getting Down to Business—Cutting the Text

1. Working in your groups, cut each speech down to five lines—the most important five lines. YOU get to decide what "important" means here; have spirited conversations about which are the most important five lines.

2. Below your cut scripts, write a brief defense of your group's choice.

3. As a group, select an image—any kind of image—that best reflects each five-line nugget. Consider:
   - What sort of emotion does the language of the passage evoke?
   - What does this emotion look like?
   - Who is Othello at the end? What is the lasting image that you want audiences to have of Othello?

4. Let's share out.

Part Three: Oral Reflection

1. Based on Othello's words and choices, how has he changed over the course of the scene? Why has this change come now? Does Othello surprise you? Why or why not? Does Othello "deserve" to determine his own story? Think about these questions as we do rounds:

2. Each of you start with the prompt and give us one sentence.
   - I noticed . . .
   - I wondered . . .
   - I learned . . . about myself.

Here's What Just Happened in Class

- Students made connections between monologues to analyze Othello's character at the end.

- Students collaborated to cut Shakespeare's text and, in doing so, read the text closely and analyzed (or argued) the value and effects of language.

- Students discovered the power of an image and added their own voice and interests to the classroom.

RESOURCE #4.4A

Mr. Hubert Carter as Othello and Miss Tita Brand as Desdemona in a production of
Othello. 1905 drawing by Max Cowper.

RESOURCE #4.4B

Othello's Three Act 5.2 Monologues

Othello 5.2.1–24

It is the cause, it is the cause, my soul.
Let me not name it to you, you chaste stars.
It is the cause. Yet I'll not shed her blood,
Nor scar that whiter skin of hers than snow,
And smooth as monumental alabaster.   5
Yet she must die, else she'll betray more men.
Put out the light, and then put out the light.
If I quench thee, thou flaming minister,
I can again thy former light restore
Should I repent me. But once put out thy light,   10
Thou cunning'st pattern of excelling nature,
I know not where is that Promethean heat
That can thy light relume. When I have plucked (the)
    rose,
I cannot give it vital growth again.   15
It needs must wither. I'll smell (it) on the tree.
O balmy breath, that dost almost persuade
Justice to break her sword! (*He kisses her.*) One
    more, one more.
Be thus when thou art dead, and I will kill thee   20
And love thee after. One more, and (this) the last.
                              (*He kisses her.*)
So sweet was ne'er so fatal. I must weep,
But they are cruel tears. This sorrow's heavenly:
It strikes where it doth love. She wakes.

Othello 5.2 310–332

Behold, I have a weapon.   310
A better never did itself sustain
Upon a soldier's thigh. I have seen the day
That with this little arm and this good sword
I have made my way through more impediments
Than twenty times your stop. But—O vain boast!—   315
Who can control his fate? 'Tis not so now.
[Be not afraid, though you do see me weaponed.
Here is my journey's end, here is my butt
And very sea-mark of my utmost sail.
Do you go back dismayed? 'Tis a lost fear.   320
Man but a rush against Othello's breast,

And he retires. Where should Othello go?

(He looks toward the bed.)

Now, how dost thou look now? O ill-starred wench,]
Pale as thy smock, when we shall meet at compt,
This look of thine will hurl my soul from heaven,   325
And fiends will snatch at it. Cold, cold, my girl?
Even like thy chastity.—O cursèd, cursèd slave!—
Whip me, you devils,
From the possession of this heavenly sight!
Blow me about in winds, roast me in sulfur,   330
Wash me in steep-down gulfs of liquid fire!
O Desdemon! Dead, Desdemon! Dead! O, O!

Othello 5.2.397–417

Soft you. A word or two before you go.
I have done the state some service, and they
    know 't.
No more of that. I pray you in your letters,   400
When you shall these unlucky deeds relate,
Speak of me as I am. Nothing extenuate,
Nor set down aught in malice. Then must you speak
Of one that loved not wisely, but too well;
Of one not easily jealous, but being wrought,   405
Perplexed in the extreme; of one whose hand,
Like the base Judean, threw a pearl away
Richer than all his tribe; of one whose subdued
    eyes,
Albeit unused to the melting mood,   410
Drops tears as fast as the Arabian trees
Their medicinable gum. Set you down this.
And say besides, that in Aleppo once,
Where a malignant and a turbanned Turk
Beat a Venetian and traduced the state,   415
I took by th' throat the circumcisèd dog,
And smote him, thus.

(He stabs himself.)

"This Heavy Act With Heavy Heart Relate": Whose Tragedy Is It Anyway?

Here's What We're Doing Today and Why

Today, students will explore the end of the play and ask themselves the question: Whose tragedy is this? Although the play is called *The Tragedy of Othello: the Moor of Venice*, there are so many other characters throughout the play who suffer their own tragedies and deaths. Desdemona, Emilia, Roderigo, Cassio, and even Bianca have their lives turned upside down by the events that occur in *Othello* and do not have the chance to tell their stories.

After analyzing and reflecting on a character from the play, students will choose a monologue or a series of lines and create a blackout poem. A blackout poem is created by starting with an existing text, keeping portions of that original and crossing out others. Blackout poems are a form of the Folger Essential of cutting that can give new meaning to old texts. Today, students' poems will work to reveal a final message that the character sends to the audience, to themselves or to society as a whole. This is now the characters' turn to set right how history will remember them. This blackout poem will demonstrate student understanding of character and scene cutting as they work to leave in their poem a new essence and truth.

The blackout poetry that students work on today will allow them to make decisions about how they view their character. As they start to look toward their final scene work next week, students will have to understand who their characters are and what they want their audience to understand about them. The work that students do today will help to develop these skills and this understanding.

Remind them that their final projects take place all next week! We're reminding you too! Get a jump on all that will occur next week by reading **RESOURCE #5.1A** at the end of this lesson.

Agenda (one 45-minute period)

- ❏ Part One—Introduction: 5 minutes
- ❏ Part Two—Blackout Poetry Work: 30 minutes
- ❏ Part Three—Debrief: 10 minutes

What Will I Need?

- Copies of the play, or monologues, soliloquies, or scenes that include Desdemona, Emilia, Roderigo, Cassio, or Bianca from which students can select their speeches. You select!

How Should I Prepare?

- Have copies of these speeches available for students, sorted into piles based on character.

- Assign students to work in pairs (if you'd like to and they'd like to).
- Have pencils and black markers at the ready!

Here's What Students Hear (From You) and (Then What They'll) Do

Part One: Introduction

Look at the character list from the play. What characters do you believe have faced tragedy in this play? List them. What characters do you think are the most tragic? Is there one that you are particularly sympathetic toward? Why do you feel this way?

Part Two: Blackout Poetry Work

1. Choose a character from the play that you found to be particularly tragic who is NOT named Othello. Students might consider Desdemona, Emilia, Roderigo, Cassio, or Bianca.

2. Look through these speeches for those characters and read through them with a pencil in hand. What word, phrase, or general idea do you like? Circle them on your page lightly for now.

3. Then, write down those words in order on a separate sheet of paper. Read them aloud. [**TEACHER NOTE:** If students need joining words ("a," "and," "the"), have them jump back into the text to find these words.]

4. When you have worked through your drafts, box or outline the words that you plan to keep with a dark marker. Remember to erase pencil lines around words you are no longer using!

5. Using a dark marker, black out the rest of the text, making sure to leave the words you need for your poem and your drawings. If it's easier to read that way, write out your poem in its entirety on a separate sheet.

Part Three: Group Share-out and Reflection

1. Let's share your blackout poetry!

2. General question: Did you learn anything new about your character? What new insight did you learn about your character?

3. Let's close with some rounds.

   a. I wonder . . .

   b. I appreciated . . .

   c. Something I learned about myself is . . .

Here's What Just Happened in Class

- Students analyzed characters and their own relationship to them.

- Students made Shakespeare their own by relating thoughts and feelings expressed in the play and their own interpretation.

- Shakespeare's minor(ish) characters took center stage.

- Students used cutting to close-read and make arguments about what is important about a minor character based on the character's own words.

- Students closely read to determine the various perspectives of minor characters in the play.

Teacher's Overview

Introducing the Final Week and the Final Project:
Make *Othello* Your Own

Final Project's Learning Goals

This project is the culmination of everything your students have been doing all unit long. Students will work in groups to make a scene or monologue from *Othello* entirely their own.

By the end of this project, every student will have:

- Pulled together all the pieces of this unit, particularly essential practices like cutting a scene, choral reading, creating a promptbook, and 3D Lit—all in order to get inside of and create a scene from anywhere in the play.

- Moved collaboratively through a complex process of reading, rereading, editing, adapting, embodying, imagining, re-editing, rehearsing, performing, deciding, and defending.

- Used the text to make choices about how to edit, adapt, and stage the scene.

- Performed their original interpretation of the *Othello* scene for an audience.

- Written and presented a group rationale for the text-based decisions that led to this performance (edits, additions, staging, etc.).

- Written a brief personal reflection on the experience of completing this project.

- Grappled with the whole play (Acts 1–5) through work in class up to now and collaborative work on their own scenes.

Both the students and you, the teacher, should walk away with resounding evidence that everyone in your class can make meaning from Shakespeare's language—from complex texts—on their own.

Advice and Reminders

Time. This learning experience is designed to take roughly 5 class periods of 45 minutes each. However, depending on your teaching context, it might take a longer or shorter amount of time. For example, this plan is written with one day for final performances, but if you need more time and have the time, take more time!

Chaos. Since it's all about turning the language and the learning over to the students, you can expect the process to get somewhat messy and noisy. As long as students are making *their own way* through their scenes, it's all good. As you have been doing right along, resist the urge to explain the text to your students. Trust the process—and trust your students to ask questions, find answers, create interpretations, and make meaning on their own, as they have been doing. (If they don't do this, then they're missing the point of the project.) Throughout this process and this week, students are tracking their cutting, adding, and promptbooking decisions and preparing to present, along with their scene performance, an oral defense of their key decisions.

Time and Less Chaos. It works out best if you can decide how much time your schedule allows you for the final performances and scene rationales on the final day of the project. Then work backwards to schedule your groups within that time.

An example: If you have 45 minutes of class time and 20 students, you might have 5 performing groups with 4 students each. That could mean that each group would have 7–8 minutes to share their work (their performance + then defense of their decisions). 8 minutes x 5 groups = 40 minutes, leaving 5 minutes for a whole-class reflection round. If this feels tight to you, give each group 7 minutes.

Flexibility and Creativity. You'll see that on the menu of scenes for this project, some scenes involve more than 4 actors, and some fewer than 4 actors. Students will add their own creativity to the mix by double-casting parts, or using other means to make sure they have full participation. This can work as well if students want to work on monologues. Interpretations of scenes should be the students' own.

Space. Giving students an area to rehearse and perform is essential to making this assessment work. Consider booking the library, auditorium, or even the gym so students have plenty of room to practice. If that is not possible, consider utilizing the hallways or sectioning off the classroom. Students need space to move.

Suggested Guidance on Assessing the Projects: A Seven-Point Checklist

1. Does the performance demonstrate a grasp of what the characters are saying and wanting?

2. Does the performance make strategic use of voice and body to convey effective tone and feeling?

3. Does the defense summarize the scene clearly, concisely, and accurately?

4. Does the defense comment on the scene's importance in the overall play and our world today?

5. Does the defense justify key decisions to cut, add, and perform language in this particular way? Is there strong and relevant textual evidence for this performance overall?

6. Does the defense describe how this process shaped new or different understandings of this play?

7. Does the personal reflection consider specific things that the student has learned, contributed, and discovered?

WEEK FIVE: LESSON 1

Your Final Projects!

Here's What We're Doing This Week and Why

Today kicks off the culminating project, the student-driven process of making Shakespeare thoroughly their own by collaborating on creating for each other scenes and monologues from *Othello*. By the end of today's lesson, students will understand what's expected of them and why—both as individuals and as project groups. They will also have gathered with their group mates and their assigned scene for this project. Although we've divided the final project into 5 days, it's really one unified, cumulative process, so please make whatever pacing adjustments your students need. Different groups might be at different steps of the process on different days, and that's okay.

What Will I Need?

- Final Project: The Teacher Overview – **RESOURCE #5.1A** (Perhaps you got an early start and have read this already!)

- Final Project: The Student Overview and Assignment – **RESOURCE #5.1B**

- The menu of suggested *Othello* scenes for groups to work up – **RESOURCE #5.1C** These scenes range from short ones (50 lines) to very long ones that will need major cutting (200 lines). You will expect MUCH more from the groups who take on the projects with fewer lines—in terms of memorization, movement, and general understanding and performance. If students prefer other scenes, they should be encouraged to do so. If some students have struggled through the unit, they might appreciate working on scenes that you've already worked on in class because they will be familiar with them.

How Should I Prepare?

- Make copies of the student overview and assignment for everyone in class.

- Make a plan for grouping students if you'd like to do that, rather than let them choose their own groups.

- Figure out how much time students will have for performing their scenes and offering their defense so you can let them know today. (See Teacher Overview, **RESOURCE #5.1A**.)

- Prepare yourself to get out of the way and let students figure things out on their own. You're assessing their ability to do exactly that.

- Reach out to teachers to give students an authentic audience. If you are in a school with younger grades, consider inviting these classes to come and watch students perform.

Agenda (one 45-minute period)

- ❏ Part One—Intro to the assignment and scene menu: 20 minutes

- ❏ Part Two—Groups meet for the first time: 25 minutes

Here's What Students Hear (From You) and (Then What They'll) Do

Part One: Project Introduction

- Give students the project assignment – **RESOURCE #5.1B** – and go through it together.

- Check for understanding with reflection rounds:
    - I notice . . .
    - I wonder . . .
    - Assign scenes, answer any wonderings, and fill in any details that students missed.

Part Two: Group Work

Students work in their groups and get started!

Here's What Just Happened in Class

- Students met their final project and started working in groups to tackle the assignment!

- Every student read out loud some of *Othello* and worked to begin brainstorming as to what they want to do with their scene.

Teacher's Overview

Introducing the Final Week and the Final Project:
Make *Othello* Your Own

Final Project's Learning Goals

This project is the culmination of everything your students have been doing all unit long. Students will work in groups to make a scene or monologue from *Othello* entirely their own.

By the end of this project, every student will have:

- Pulled together all the pieces of this unit, particularly essential practices like cutting a scene, creating a promptbook, and 3D Shakespeare, in order to get inside of and create a scene from anywhere in the play.

- Moved collaboratively through a complex process of reading, rereading, editing, adapting, embodying, imagining, re-editing, rehearsing, performing, deciding, and defending.

- Used the text to make choices about how to edit, adapt, and stage the scene.

- Performed their original interpretation of the *Othello* scene for an audience.

- Written and presented a group rationale for the text-based decisions that led to this performance (edits, additions, staging, etc.).

- Written a brief personal reflection on the experience of completing this project.

- Grappled with the whole play (Acts 1 through 5) through work in class up to now and collaborative work on their own scenes.

Both the students and you, the teacher, should walk away with resounding evidence that everyone in your class can make meaning from Shakespeare's language—from complex texts—on their own.

Advice and Reminders:

Time. This learning experience is designed to take roughly 5 class periods of 45 minutes each. However, depending on your teaching context, it might take a longer or shorter time. For example, this plan is written with one day for final performances, but if you need more time and have the time, take more time!

Chaos. Since it's all about turning the language and the learning over to the students, you can expect the process to get somewhat messy and noisy. As long as students are making *their own way* through their scenes, it's all good. As you have been doing right along, resist the urge to explain the text to your students. Trust the process—and trust your students to ask questions, find answers, create interpretations, and make meaning on their own, as they have been doing. (If they don't do this, then they're missing the point of the project.) Throughout this process and this week, students are tracking their cutting, adding, and promptbooking decisions and preparing to present, along with their scene performance, an oral defense of their key decisions.

Time and Less Chaos. It works out best if you can decide how much time your schedule allows you for the final performances and scene rationales on the final day of the project. Then work backwards to schedule your groups within that time.

An example: If you have 45 minutes of class time and 20 students, you might have 5 performing groups with 4 students each. That could mean that each group would have 7–8 minutes to share their work (their performance + then defense of their decisions). 8 minutes x 5 groups = 40 minutes, leaving 5 minutes for a whole-class reflection round. If this feels tight to you, give each group 7 minutes.

Flexibility and Creativity. You'll see that on the menu of scenes for this project, some scenes involve more than four actors, and some fewer than four actors. Students will add their own creativity to the mix by double-casting parts, or using other means to make sure they have full participation. This can work as well if students want to work on monologues. Interpretations of scenes should be the students' own.

Space. Giving students an area to rehearse and perform is essential to making this assessment work. Consider booking the library, auditorium, or even the gymnasium so students have plenty of room to practice. If that is not possible, consider utilizing the hallways or sectioning off the classroom. Students need space to move.

Suggested Guidance on Assessing the Projects: A Seven-Point Checklist

1. Does the performance demonstrate a grasp of what the characters are saying and wanting?

2. Does the performance make strategic use of voice and body to convey effective tone and feeling?

3. Does the defense summarize the scene clearly, concisely, and accurately?

4. Does the defense comment on the scene's importance in the overall play and our world today?

5. Does the defense justify key decisions to cut, add, and perform language in this particular way? Is there strong and relevant textual evidence for this performance overall?

6. Does the defense describe how this process shaped new or different understandings of this play?

7. Does the personal reflection consider specific things that the student has learned, contributed, and discovered?

Student's Overview and Assignment

Introducing the Final Week and the Final Project:
Make *Othello* Your Own

You will work in groups to bring a scene from *Othello* to life. This project is the culmination of everything you have been doing all unit long, and you will be demonstrating all that you have learned all this week as you make these scenes your own!

By the end of this project, you will have:

- Put together all the pieces of this unit, particularly essential practices like cutting a scene, creating a promptbook, and 3D Lit, in order to get inside of and create a scene or monologue from *Othello.*

- Moved collaboratively through a complex process of reading, rereading, editing, adapting, embodying, imagining, re-editing, rehearsing, performing, deciding, and defending.

- Used the text to make choices about how to edit, adapt, and stage the scene.

- Performed your original interpretation of the scene for an audience.

- Written and presented a group rationale for the text-based decisions that led to this performance (edits, additions, staging, etc.).

- Written a brief personal reflection on the experience of completing this project.

- Grappled with the whole play (Acts 1–5) through work in class up to now and collaborative work through one of the scenes.

You, your classmates, and your teacher will walk away with resounding evidence that YOU can make meaning from Shakespeare's language—from complex texts—on your own.

What You Will Produce

1. A performed scene from *Othello* (in a group)

2. A defense of your scene, delivered orally and in writing (in a group)

3. A personal reflection on this project (from you, as an individual)

Your Action Steps

1. **Get your group and scene assignment** from your teacher.

2. Next, before anything else: With your group, **dive deeply into your scene or monologue**. Read it out loud as a group, just as we have done in class. Take notes on all of this—these will come in handy later. Collaboratively as a group, figure out:

   – What's happening in the scene

> – What the characters are saying
>
> – What each of the characters wants
>
> – Why the scene is important in the play
>
> – Why someone should care about this scene today

3. Next, **consider the end goal**: your group is making a scene of **X** minutes and an oral defense of the scene that is no longer than **X** minutes. Your teacher will tell you the timing that you—like any group of actors—must work with. Keep this in mind as you work through the scene.

4. Next, work to **be directors and put the scene on its feet**. Each member of the group should be **creating a promptbook** for the scene along the way so that you're all working from the same script with the same notes. Together, make—and note—decisions about the following and be prepared to explain to your audience what in the text (and in your personal experience of reading it) motivated you to cut, add, and perform as you did:

   - **Cutting the scene.** Perhaps you must cut it so that it fits your time limit and still makes sense. What must stay? What can go?

   - **Locating the scene.** Where is it happening? What does this place look like? Feel like? Smell like? Sound like? How do you know this?

   - **Adding to the scene.** You may want to choose 1–2 outside texts to mash up with your scene. If you do, what is gained by putting these texts into your Shakespeare scene? What made you choose this/these text/texts? Why and where do they work best? If you choose to add outside texts, be sure that at least 80% of your scene is *Othello*.

   - **Getting ready to perform the scene.** Cast the parts. Which of you plays whom? Every group member must speak. What does each character want and think and feel? How can the audience tell? Who is moving where on what line, and why? Get on your feet and start moving, because some of these questions are answered when you get a scene on its feet. As you know, this is not about acting talent; it is about knowing what you are saying and doing as you bring life to this scene.

   - **As you go, you're documenting your decisions and preparing your oral defense of the scene.** What are the most significant or original decisions your group made? What drove those decisions? Let the audience into your interpretive process, your minds, ever so concisely. Your defense should involve every group member and do the following:

     – Summarize your scene

     – Comment on the scene's importance in the overall play

     – Justify your cutting, adding, and performing choices with textual evidence

     – Conclude by describing how the process of preparing this performance shaped new or different understandings of *Othello*

5. **Rehearse.** Yes, you should memorize your lines, though you can ask someone to serve as your prompter, as we think Shakespeare's company might have done. Repeat: This is not about acting talent.

6. **Perform your scene and present your scene rationale** during your scheduled class period. After your performance, present your rationale for your scene. As with your performance, every group member must speak. Focus on just the most significant decisions and stick to your time limit. We will all watch all the final project scenes together so that we can celebrate wrapping up *Othello* with YOUR voices.

7. At that time, you will **submit the 2 written documents**:
   – The written version of your group's defense of your scene.
   – An individual reflection (400–500 words) reflecting on the experience—both the process and what you feel were your own contributions to the project.

RESOURCE #5.1C

Menu: Suggested Scenes from *Othello*

ACTS & SCENES	LINES	# OF CHARACTERS
Act 1, scene 1	74–160	3–4
Act 1, scene 1	161–206	3
Act 1, scene 2	65–123	3–5
Act 1, scene 3	149–196	4
Act 1, scene 3	343–447	2
Act 2, scene 1	234–307	2
Act 2, scene 3	1–48	3
Act 2, scene 3 MAKE AGGRESSIVE CUTS	48–284*	6
Act 3, scene 3	321–382	4
Act 3, scene 3	435–490	2
Act 4, scene 1	126–163	3
Act 5, scene 2	204–435	7–8

Your Final Project: Making *Othello* Your Own

Here's What We're Doing and Why

We're here! Groups are making their way through the final project this week. They are working on scenes, demonstrating as they go what they have learned in terms of making the language, characters, and action their own—all infused with their own energy and creativity. And they are presenting as we finish up *Othello*.

Agenda for Lessons 2, 3, and 4

LESSON 2:

❏ Introduction: 10 minutes

❏ Cutting the scene: 35 minutes

LESSON 3:

❏ Introduction: 10 minutes

❏ Adding outside texts if you choose to, and promptbooking the newly edited scene: 35 minutes

LESSON 4:

❏ Warm-up with a scene cheer: 10 minutes

❏ Rehearsing the scene and writing the scene rationale: 35 minutes

What Will I Need for These Three Lessons?

• Some print copies of the Folger Shakespeare edition of the play for student reference

• A few dictionaries or Shakespeare glossaries for student reference (if available)

• Space and time for students to make their way through this project

• Strength to resist the urge to explain or interpret the text for students (you're a pro by now)

• Access to outside books, songs, poems, films, etc., if they choose to add outside material to their scene

• A discreet eye to observe students as they work

How Should I Prepare for These Three Lessons?

• As long as every student understands the task at hand, you're good. Students are doing the hard work now!

Lesson 2: Here's What Students Hear (From You) and (Then What They'll) Do

Part One: Warm-up

1. Choose your favorite line from your scene.

2. Count off by 4. Meet with the other students with the same number.

3. Toss your lines in a circle; everyone should say their line three times (say it differently each time!).

4. Discuss as a class: Given the lines you heard in your circle, what do you think is happening in the scenes we are performing? Which delivery of your line felt like the best fit for your character or scene? Why?

Part Two: Group Work

Groups are reading, rereading, and cutting their final scenes. They are also cooperating to compose a rationale for their unique performance of the scene. For a closer look at the steps in this process, please refer to the Student Overview and Assignment – **RESOURCE 5.1B**.

Students may feel the need to take this work home with them, especially the two writing tasks: the group rationale and the personal reflection. Check in with your students each class to see where they are in the process, and help them set realistic goals for homework (if necessary) and classwork. If you need to push due dates for the writing, we recommend that you do so. Performance dates, though, should be upheld whenever possible to make sure that there is a clear end in sight for the unit.

Lesson 3: Here's What Students Hear (From You) and (Then What They'll) Do

Part One: Warm-up

1. In your groups, agree on a song that best represents your scene.

2. Discuss with your small group. Share with the class.

3. If you can, play a snippet from the song!

Part Two: Group Work

Groups are cutting, adapting, promptbooking, and rehearsing their final scenes. If they are including an outside text(s), they should decide what and how today. For a closer look at the steps in this process, please refer to the Student Overview and Assignment – **RESOURCE #5.1B**.

Once again, check in with your students each class to see where they are in the process, help them set realistic goals for homework and classwork, and see that they have a plan to complete the two writing tasks.

Lesson 4: Here's What Students Hear (From You) and (Then What They'll) Do

Part One: Warm-up

1. In your groups, come up with a group cheer. The cheer must include:

    a. Three words from the scene or monologue

    b. Two arm movements

2. Groups have 5 minutes to practice and then share with the class.

Part Two: Group Work

Groups are rehearsing their final scenes. They are also cooperating to compose a rationale for their unique performance of their scene. For a closer look at the steps in this process, please refer to the Student Overview and Assignment – **RESOURCE #5.1B**.

Students typically need to work at home on these, especially the two writing tasks: the group rationale and the personal reflection. Check in with your students each class to see where they are in the process, and help them set realistic goals for homework and classwork.

Here's What Just Happened in Class During These Three Classes

- You observed a class full of students in a state of flow, deeply engaged in the process of making a scene from *Othello* their own!

- You watched peers help one another by asking good questions, building comprehension, citing textual evidence, and encouraging creativity.

The Final Project: Your Own *Othello*, Performed!

Here's What We're Doing and Why

It's showtime! Watch and listen as your students demonstrate their ability to grapple with, respond to, and perform Shakespeare's language. Hear why they staged things as they did. Celebrate how far your students have come, not just as Shakespeareans but as thinkers and readers and makers. Don't forget to save time for a whole-class reflection round after all the performances. This is often just as enlightening as the scenes themselves, if not more so.

Agenda

- ❏ Groups get organized: 5 minutes
- ❏ Scenes performed and defenses presented: 40 minutes
- ❏ Whole-class reflection: 10 minutes

What Will I Need?

- Space and time for all groups to present their performances and rationales

- A notepad or digital doc to take notes on all the great learning you're witnessing. These notes will come in handy when you provide student feedback. (Revisit the seven-point checklist and the learning goals of the final project when it's time for feedback.)

- Space and time for everyone to gather in a circle for a reflection round

How Should I Prepare?

- Create and share the "run of show" for today. At the beginning of class, groups should know when they're on.

- Arrange your space so everyone can see each scene. A giant circle is our favorite format.

- It's always nice to have a lighthearted but clear way to call "time" on a scene. Some teachers rely on a phone timer. Your call.

- Will any other classes stop by to watch?

Here's What Students Will Do

Part One

- Groups get organized. Students meet in their groups to organize props or make quick, last-minute changes for their scene.

Part Two: Performances

- Each group presents their work to thunderous applause.
- Collect whatever project documentation you need to assess student learning.

Part Three: Reflection Rounds

Respond to the following prompts: "Just thinking just about your work this week, including this performance experience, let's do these rounds."

- I noticed . . .
- I learned . . .
- I learned about myself . . .

Here's What Just Happened in Class

- Massive learning in action, all set up by you. WOW!

Teaching Shakespeare—and
Othello—with English Learners

Christina Porter

I am Christina Porter, and for the past twenty years I have worked in an urban school community right outside of Boston, Massachusetts. I began as an English teacher, then a literacy coach, and currently I am the district curriculum director for the humanities. I first started working with English Learners in 2006 when I became a literacy coach. Prior to that, I had little experience with these phenomenal students.

Also prior to working with them, I knew the general assumptions about ELs. For as long as they have sat in U.S. classrooms, ELs most often have been considered "other," having many "deficits" that need to be overcome. The "deficits" tend to be their native language and culture—seen as roadblocks that should be surmounted so that EL students can more closely match prevailing assumptions of "American" culture—white, middle-class, and English-speaking. In my work with EL students, I soon learned that this mindset can manifest itself in many ugly ways in schools, and that can be both culturally and academically destructive.

Something I observed early on was that while our white, middle-class, English-speaking students were reading Shakespeare—the real thing, not that watered-down summarized stuff—our English Learners were not. Not even a watered-down version of Shakespeare! By "real Shakespeare" I mean his words in all their glorious Early Modern English (both with the full text of a play as well as in edited scenes from a play). Initially, I had the incorrect assumption myself: I assumed, like so many others, that because students were developing English, Shakespeare was probably too difficult for them to handle. I learned that this is incorrect. What I learned instead was that once we adults dismissed our own deficit-based thinking—and allowed our EL students to read, create, design, and imagine—the results were tremendous, with Shakespeare as well as with many other complex texts.

Coinciding with my start as a literacy coach, I spent a summer at the Folger Library's Teaching Shakespeare Institute. I learned about so many of the student-centered, get-them-on-their-feet methods that are one of the backbones of this book. As the new literacy coach at the high school, I was so excited to get into a classroom and use these, especially because I had the unique opportunity to work with many teachers in the building. One of the first colleagues to reach out was an English as a Second Language (ESL) teacher. We met to brainstorm, and I described how I had spent my summer at the Folger Library learning all of these innovative methods of engaging students. She was immediately onboard. Specifically, she wanted to tackle Shakespeare (again, REAL Shakespeare). Over the course of several years, we taught many plays together, and I did the same with other colleagues in the ESL department. Our ELs consistently destroyed any concern I or others could have had about their ability to read and perform something as intricate and complex as Shakespeare. Just one example: one of the first things I learned was that these students are uniquely attuned to the intricacy of language; it's how they exist on a daily basis! Sometimes when teaching a play with my native speakers, I found that they would want to rush. In this rushing, they would miss the depth and beauty of the words. ELs, on the other hand, take time with language—with the word, the line, the speech, and the scene. This is only one of the many strengths these students bring to working with Shakespeare, and other authors too.

Because the Folger understands the importance of ELs, I have been asked to share some of the knowledge I've gained working with these unique, intelligent, and resilient EL students and Shakespeare. My suggestions are based on years of scholarly research regarding second language acquisition coupled with my knowledge and experience working with ELs, Shakespeare, and the Folger Method. I am excited to share both what I've taught and what I've learned from EL students!

One important and perhaps obvious note here is that English Learners are not a monolith. You may have students in your class who have had exposure to English in their native country, you may also have students who have experienced gaps in schooling, and more. Though most of this chapter is focused on ELs generally, when I have found an approach that is particularly helpful for a specific subgroup of ELs, I point that out.

I build here on principles and classroom practices that you will find throughout this book and this series. Since teachers are the busiest people on the planet, this material is organized so that you can find what you need quickly:

❑ **Part One: ELs at Home in the Folger Method**

❑ **Part Two: Shakespeare with English Learners**

❑ **Part Three: *Othello* with English Learners**

Part One: ELs at Home in the Folger Method

Many of the Folger Essentials are *already* excellent supports for ELs. Folger Essentials like choral reading, rereading, focusing on single words and lines, and then building to speeches and scenes—all of these support fluency and comprehension. In addition, these *Teaching Guides* include plot summaries and play maps, and the lesson plans include lots of other active instructional approaches.

When reading Shakespeare with ELs, I always give the option to read the scene summary or check out the play map in advance. They're both elsewhere in this book. I do this because it balances accessibility with giving them a chance to grapple with a complex text. Remember, Shakespeare borrowed most of his plots, so the plot is the least of our concern. We never want the story to become the roadblock to working with the words. The Folger Shakespeare, both in print and online, includes brief play and scene synopses for all of the plays. The play maps may be helpful to ELs who may have had interruptions in their prior schooling or ELs who have not previously read a drama. It can be another structural support to "unveil" the characters and plot. You may choose to spend some time deconstructing the structure of a piece of drama—discussing, for example, scenes, acts, and character lists. For some students, drama may be completely new; for others, this quick activity can serve as an activator of prior knowledge.

Understanding text features is a solid support for comprehension. It is easy to assume that, by high school when most students are reading this play, they have been exposed to drama, but this is not always the case, depending on the backgrounds of individual students.

Part Two: Shakespeare with English Learners

With the Folger Method as my base, I build in additional resources to support English Learners in my urban school. This is because working with ELs *is* different from working with native English speakers. Equity is removing barriers. Equity is giving students what they need to be successful. Thus, I have come to four Truths that prevail when diving into Shakespeare—and other complex texts too—with EL students:

- Truth #1: **ELs need support with classroom practices.** We cannot assume that our ELs have had the same experience in classrooms as our other students. We need to offer specific guidance and support for common classroom practices such as having a small group discussion, acting out a piece of drama, or other Folger Essentials. Being clear in our expectations, our directions, and offering scaffolds (for example, sentence starters for small-group discussions) is good for all students and essential for ELs.

- Truth #2: **ELs need additional supports in order to grapple with complex texts.** ELs are capable of reading Shakespeare. ELs also need supports for language comprehension. Important supports include chunking a scene/speech into smaller parts and using edited scenes or plays. To be clear, we always use Shakespeare's text (rather than the "simplified" versions) and we want to offer accessibility to those words through appropriate support for students who are in the process of acquiring English.

- Truth #3: **ELs need to have space for their unique language and culture to live in our classrooms.** Students' funds of knowledge are an asset, not a deficit. They need to bring their whole selves and their whole native culture to Shakespeare. This truth echoes the Folger principle about the importance of student voice.

- Truth #4: **ELs need support with the specific aspects of the English language and how words function** (individually, in a sentence, and more). This helps them to build academic vocabulary, in written as well as oral language.

Continuing from Truth #4 and parts of the Folger Method, I introduce my students to what I call the "actor's arsenal"—a toolbox of 5 elements of communication that actors (and all of us) have at their disposal in English: stress, inflection, pause, nonverbal communication, and tone. At its simplest, it looks like this, and my students appreciate this visual:

STRESS: Emphasis placed on a **WORD** (or word, or word)

INFLECTION: The way the voice goes ^{up} or _{down} when a word is pronounced

PAUSE: A break ..... in reading for emphasis

NONVERBAL COMMUNICATION: Without words, the gestures, posture, presence or absence of eye contact

TONE: The *emotional* sound in your voice

These five tools deserve attention because *they are not the same in all languages.* In some languages, some of these tools are nonexistent or used in different ways than they are in English. I have a distinct memory of teaching a lesson on tone for the first time to a class of ELs. Generally, students really enjoy practicing a word/line with varying tones of voice. In this class, I couldn't help but notice one student who had a puzzled look on his face. I didn't want to embarrass him in his small group, so I sought guidance from the ESL teacher I was working with. She explained to me that tone did not work the same way in his native language as it did in English. In some languages—Hmong, for example—tone alone literally changes the meaning of a word, while in other languages—English, for one—tone accompanied by nonverbal communication alters the subtext of a word/phrase.

When working with students who have varying language backgrounds, additional attention to tone and nonverbal communication is very helpful. I typically introduce this "arsenal" as a part of our pre-reading. Tone and Stress, the first Folger Essential, includes visuals and practice rounds, and is recommended for all students beginning their journey with Shakespeare's language. Learn more about it in the Folger Method chapter. What I describe here can be an additional and introductory support for EL students.

I often begin this communication work by asking students to consider a universal teenage dilemma—having a disagreement with your parents or caregivers. (I have found, after working with students from all over the world, that this is one of the few situations that transcends language and culture for most adolescents.) I then ask them to brainstorm all the different ways they can "show" their displeasure with words or actions. The list they generate generally includes items like volume, eye rolling, silence, additional gestures, and tone of voice. I then introduce the concept of tone vocabulary and include visuals with each element to further support comprehension. We pay particular attention to tone, as the English language offers infinite options for impacting the meaning of a word or phrase with tone alone. We define "tone" as the emotional sound in your voice, and I offer a specific list of tones for students' reference: love, hate, anger, joy, fear, and sorrow. While certainly not comprehensive of all the tones available in English, these six seem to capture the fundamentals. Students always enjoy taking a phrase like "That's great!" and applying these tones in small groups. For students coming from language backgrounds where tone is not utilized in the same way as it is in English, this activity offers additional practice in and added awareness of how tone functions in English. Using the Folger Essential, students practice with the word "Oh!," saying it in a variety of tones (happy, sad, angry, surprised, and more). Students on their own will automatically add accompanying nonverbal communication, crossing their arms if the tone is angry, for example.

In addition, you can use a film clip of a scene from a Shakespeare play to further explore tone. (There is a wide variety of clips online, or check out www.folger.edu.) Initially, I hand out to the students a copy of the scene, and I play the clip *audio only.* Students can work individually or they can work in small groups. They listen to the audio only, following along with the lines. As they listen, I instruct them to focus on one character and note any tone of voice they hear (anger, love, joy, and more). Next, we watch the scene *video only,* with no audio at all. They continue to track the same character and note any nonverbal communication. Finally, we watch the scene *with audio and video,* and add any additional notes on tone, stress, nonverbal communication, inflection, or pause. After this, students share their notes and findings in either a pair (if they have been working individually) or with another small group. Later, when we get up on our feet as a class, we are able to draw upon this kind of analysis to support our version of the play!

Part Three: *Othello* with English Learners

Two of my four truths around EL students and Shakespeare focus on students' need for additional supports when working with the English language, and on EL students' need for an invitation to include their language and culture. Born from these truths (and backed up by the Folger Method), I share here approaches and practices that I have used most frequently when reading *Othello* with EL students. You will find that these strategies are useful for all students but essential for ELs!

Truth #4—ELs need support with specific aspects of the English language—breaks down into 4 different kinds of supports:

   a. **Sensory supports**, such as visual representations, models, manipulatives, and diagrams

   b. **Graphic supports**, such as charts, timelines, and graphic organizers

   c. **Interactive supports**, such as working in pairs, or in small groups

   d. **Supports for the text**, such as summaries, guiding questions, or chunking text into smaller pieces

As our play map cues, there's A LOT going on in this play . . . from the conflicts, to the deceptions, to the issues with race and class. Therefore, we begin *Othello* with an extension of the play map—a character connections map that the students create themselves. The purpose of extending into a connections map is that it allows students to use the whole cast list to construct a deeper understanding of the full cast, where they are from, and how they are connected. Students can use the *Othello* cast list on the Folger Shakespeare website (folger.edu/Othello/read) to draw and analyze the connections between the various characters in the play, based on the descriptions in the list. This list also introduces the settings of Venice and Cyprus and hints at the rank and status of the characters . . . though more on that later!

Directions

1. Arrange students into small groups and give them *Othello*'s list of characters. They should have the *Othello* play map at hand too, but they will do bigger, grander ones!

2. Provide each group member with a large sheet of paper for their character maps—11 x 17 is great.

3. Prior to beginning, have students define: **Moor, Venetian/Venice**, and **Cyprus**. My students generally just use a quick web search!

4. Beginning as a class, read aloud the first character and character description (if there is a description). In the Folger list, the first character is "OTHELLO, a Moorish general in the Venetian army." On your large visual for the class, draw some kind of figure to represent Othello. Instruct students to do the same on their maps.

5. The next character listed is "DESDEMONA, a Venetian lady" (and I add *"wife to Othello"*). Somewhere on the board, draw a stick person and label it "Desdemona," and write the character description below. Draw a line to connect her to her husband (write an "M" to indicate married over the line).

6. Explain to students that whenever a connection is described between characters (son of . . . wife of . . . friend of . . . , etc.), they should draw some form of line to indicate that on their map.

7. Now that students have the first few characters mapped—and they have the play map to give them confidence—explain to them that they should continue to create their maps in their small groups based on the character descriptions and connections.

8. Circulate around the room as students work, answering questions and checking their maps.

Working this way, the students are introduced to all the characters and are connecting them with each other themselves. They are also introduced to the characters' identifying factors (rank, marital status, etc.). This map serves as a reference while reading the play. I next ask students to work in their small groups to come up with the different categories that they can assign to the characters at this point. The general list includes the following: military rank, political rank, social rank (class, race, or gender), and geographic location. We arrange the characters by rank to begin thinking about who has power (depending on how we are sorting).

Military Rank	Political Rank
1. Othello (General)	1. Duke of Venice
2. Cassio (lieutenant)	2. Brabantio (senator)
3. Iago (ancient)	3. Venetian Senators, Montano (an official)

Inevitably, students notice that only Othello is defined by a term many of them have not seen before working with this character list, "Moor." Here we begin our most consistent conversation for the rest of the play—the focus on identity. We break identity into:

- your public vs. private self,

- your reputation, and

- the assignment of "other" by your others.

The assignment of "other" by your others is the idea that when you look and/or sound different from those around you, those folks may decide that you are "other," or different from them based solely on how they perceive you are not like them. *Othello* is a play about relationships, betrayal, honor, character, and the role of "the other" in a society. Painful to acknowledge is the fact that many of my students—based on their native language, their culture, and/or the color of their skin—are "othered" on a daily basis. So we take multiple opportunities to examine this play and the characters through those student experiences.

To start the conversation on this topic, I introduce the following terms:

- **Endonym,** the term folks from a place use to identify themselves or the place they live in. "Venezia," for example, is the term Italians use for "Venice."

- **Exonym,** the term folks from outside of a place use to refer to that place or to the people who live there. For example, in the U.S. we call Deutschland "Germany." Folks from western or southern states have referred to people from the Northeast as "Yankees." This is not a term most folks in the Northeast use to refer to themselves.

I then share that the word "Moor" was invented by Europeans during the Middle Ages to describe folks from northwestern areas of Africa, Sicily, and Malta who were Muslim. Many of these folks were members of the Berber or Arab peoples. Many of these people were Black. This term can have a negative feeling/meaning associated with it depending on who is using it and how it is used. It is not really used in modern day. I then ask students to create personal organizers where they name themselves in the center. Around their name, I ask them to divide the paper in half. On one side we label "Endonyms"; on the other side we label "Exonyms." On one half, they list words that identify who they are. I ask them to use their native language if they prefer and include things like this: where they were born, where they have lived, how close friends and family describe them, their roles (son, daughter, etc.), the language(s) they speak. On the exonym side they list how strangers describe them. On this side I have seen things ranging from silly—"they know my style is FIRE"—to devastating stereotypes and even slurs. It is important to say that we engage in this activity at a point in the year where we have developed a safe and supportive classroom environment. Regardless, students are given the option to share their personal organizer with a small group or with me. Either way, we practice using our oral language to share what they have written/illustrated in a small group. I always end this activity with a quick write, asking them to share how they are feeling about what they created. To be clear, my students are resilient, powerful, and brilliant. Even if they have experience of being "othered," most are strong in their identity and proud of who they are, as they should be. If students need any additional support, I always follow up.

After students have had the chance to think about their own identity in relation to how others see them and how they see themselves, we look to examine how characters in the play see Othello. I ask the guiding question: **Is Othello seen as a person (a unique individual), is he seen only by his culture and his race, or is he seen somewhere in the middle?** How Othello is seen by others is essential to the acting of the play and also gives students a lens into the character's identity. I begin with this question prior to reading 1.1, and continue to revisit it throughout the play. This is a really good ticket-to-leave question because after 1.1, Othello is never referred to by his name, only as "the Moor."

We use the tools provided by the Folger Shakespeare online (folger.edu/Othello/read) to learn from the language of the play and analyze how Othello is treated and described by others. The Folger Shakespeare online allows students to search a text to show how many times a word or phrase is used. I remember when I first asked students to do this, one student noticed that Othello's real name is used 22 times in the play, yet the word "Moor" is used to refer to him 45 times. The student added, "Usually behind his back, Miss, like when he's not even there."

I created the organizer below for 1.1 to allow students the chance to dig deeper into the focus question mentioned above ("Is Othello seen as a person . . ."). For this organizer, I filled in the scene and act as well as the context. Students use the "search" feature in the upper right-hand corner of the Folger online edition of the play to cut and paste the lines that mention either "Othello" or "Moor." Alternatively, you can fill out the entire organizer and then ask students to examine how Othello is being talked about in this scene. Students always find that his name is never spoken. He is simply referred to as "the Moor."

Scene/act	Speaker/context	Quote
1.1	**Iago, Roderigo, Brabantio**—in the opening scene of the play, **Iago and Roderigo** plan to go tell **Desdemona's** father she has run off with **Othello**.	**Iago:** Now, sir, be judge yourself, / Whether I in any just term am affined / To love the **Moor**. **Iago:** Were I the **Moor**, I would not be Iago **Iago:** I am one, sir, that comes to tell you your daughter / and the **Moor** are now making the beast with two backs.

| | | **Roderigo:** to the gross clasps of a lascivious **Moor**— |
| | | **Brabantio:** Now, Roderigo, Where didst thou see her? O unhappy girl! With the **Moor**, say'st thou? Who would be a father! How didst thou know 'twas she? O she deceives me |

Inspired by my student who noticed the way Othello is spoken about behind his back, I have students pull a series of lines (like the ones above) and create a performance to help them answer the question "How is Othello seen?" To do this, you can have students search "Moor" and "Othello" in the play, or you can present them with a page of lines (including the speaker and a quick context). They create their performance, and they have come up with brilliant staging such as having the actor playing Othello stand with his back to the audience or having the characters who speak about him negatively wear masks when they are behind his back, which they quickly remove when he enters the stage. They have also spoken some of the lines that include "Moor" as an incantation—"lascivious Moor, cruel Moor, lusty Moor"—in a whisper until the character playing Othello enters the stage. Kids are so very brilliant!

Othello offers a unique place to examine who we really are, and who we are perceived to be by others. This is something that all adolescents can relate to on a personal level. In teaching this play with ELs, you have the opportunity to allow them to use their unique, lived experience to really understand these characters. My students know that I love Bob Marley. He often plays in the background as we work. One of my favorite songs is "Redemption Song," one of Marley's final songs, which speaks of many things, including freedom from oppression. While we cannot control what the other characters do to Othello, or how they shape his fate as an "other," we can imagine a different ending for him. I often end the play by revisiting the idea of how we identify ourselves vs. how others see us. I have students work in a small group and make a T-chart of Othello. On one side, they list some of the ways Othello is treated/described by others. On the other side, they list who they believe he really was. I have seen responses including "leader," "intelligent," and "three-dimensional." We strip away the misunderstandings and static characterization of him by his peers and sing his redemption song as a class.

Teaching Shakespeare—including *Othello*—to Students with Learning Differences

Roni DiGenno

I am Roni DiGenno, a Special Education teacher with ten years' experience teaching ninth- through twelfth-grade English in a District of Columbia public high school. My students' reading levels range from pre-primer to college level and their special education classifications include specific learning disabilities, ADHD, auditory disabilities, and autism, as well as intellectual and emotional disabilities. I teach self-contained, pull-out classes, each of about fifteen students, all with IEPs Sometimes I have a teaching assistant, but most often I do not.

I love teaching. I love my students. And I love teaching Shakespeare to my students. I put to use what I have learned at the Folger; I use Shakespeare to inspire my students to believe in themselves. Most importantly, my students begin to see themselves as learners because I trust them with the hard stuff, the challenging content. I believe we can do it together, and my students know this. My passion for teaching these kids, who at times seem unreachable, comes from my own experience growing up with a reading difficulty. I could not sound out words, but this had nothing to do with my value or my intellect. My students, and all students, deserve the best, most engaging, intellectually stimulating lessons possible.

Shakespeare Rewrites How Students See Themselves and Learning

For the past several years, I have taught exclusively some of the most difficult students in my school—those with very large learning gaps, usually reading 5–8 years below grade level, and with emotional disturbances that make it difficult to build positive peer and adult relationships. They arrive in my classroom plagued with low expectations of themselves and of school because for years other people have had low expectations of them. They are used to passing just by showing up and doing minimal work. Some have been through the criminal justice system, which adds another layer of low expectations. My first priority is to help my students see themselves as capable and valued members of our classroom community. I do this by teaching lessons that empower them—lessons based on the Folger's philosophy. As a result, my students grow in exciting and surprising ways that no one could have anticipated.

I teach students like Armando, who had serious trust issues. He cut class frequently and was involved in groups that negatively influenced him in school. He repeated grades because he refused to do the work and he cursed teachers out regularly. In addition to being in and out of the criminal justice system, he was also a target of violent crime, which left him hospitalized for weeks and suffering from post-traumatic stress disorder. Through our class's collaborative work using Folger methods, Armando slowly began to discover and enjoy his strengths. He felt welcomed into the learning process and started to trust himself and others. He eventually became a peer leader who helped facilitate lessons.

I also teach Martin, a student who had such severe dyslexia that early on in my class he was reading at a kindergarten level. He was withdrawn and shied away from participating for fear of judgment. Here again, by incorporating Folger principles and practices, I was able to give Martin the safe learning environment that he needed and the confidence to try reading aloud. He learned to trust his peers and he began to take risks—reading parts, participating, and giving amazing insight into discussion topics.

The Folger Method supports students like Armando and Martin, who have vastly different learning needs but who may also be in the same class. The teaching strategies offer students multiple entry points—tactical, visual, and aural—through which to engage and enjoy complex texts. Differentiation and scaffolding are built into the Folger's interactive lessons so students build a positive association with challenging texts. This is hugely important for students with learning differences and emotional difficulties. If content or concepts are overwhelming, or not taught in a way that they can grasp them, students will build a negative association. No one wants to struggle or feel like they can't learn something, which is often the root cause of behavior issues within classrooms. The Folger Method meets students' social and emotional learning needs through building a supportive and collaborative classroom community. Through the process, students begin to work through conflict, solve problems, and accept and support each other's learning differences.

How the Folger Method Works for Students with IEPs

·In the Folger Method and *Othello* Lessons sections of this book, you'll find the Folger Essentials that will throw your students right into the text through powerful practices like tossing words and phrases, two-line scenes, choral reading, and 3D Shakespeare. Each Essential gives students exposure to the language and removes a barrier to learning and comprehension. Each builds on the others, increasing cognitive demand. Students master each step before moving to the next—words before lines, lines before scenes, choral reading before acting and reading parts solo. They don't feel left behind because they learn the content and the skills to understand it simultaneously.

Every year, my students look forward to my unit on Shakespeare. Typically about ten weeks long, the unit allows us to slow down and dig into the text. Instead of skipping over difficult parts, we want to conquer them! It is important for us to embrace the struggle because it is an inevitable part of the learning process. In the Folger work, struggle is about joyful investigation and thinking hard together rather than a feeling of inadequacy. Students question, try out, and connect with the words and each other, and so they learn that there is no one right answer but rather a whole new way to discover a text. The Essentials get the language in the students' mouths, encourage collaboration, and shift focus away from the teacher so that students can practice navigating themselves through their learning. It's a different way of teaching and a different way of learning. At first, they are hesitant: they resist, they laugh, they feel weird, they are unsure, they can't believe they are talking this much in class—and I am encouraging all of it. Within a week or two, students are more willing to experiment and take risks with the language by reading really strange words they have never seen or heard before. And soon, students are reading Shakespeare and enjoying it.

Reading Shakespeare can be a great equalizer. While scholars and directors and actors never tire of decoding, interpreting, and defining Shakespeare, the truth is that no one knows exactly what Shakespeare really meant. He left no diary or notes. Everyone is entitled to their own interpretation. We also have no idea how the words were spoken, because we have no audio recordings of the play performances in the Globe Theatre in 1600. The "funny" English (my students' term) in Shakespeare's works puts us all on the same playing field. Be vulnerable, mess up some words, and have fun! The students will ask, "How do you say this word?" and my only response is, "Not sure, let's figure it out." It's okay to do your best and sound "funny." We are all in this together, and repeating that idea to students builds bridges.

The Folger Method gives students the scaffolding and tools needed to launch them from struggling readers to invested readers. Martin, my student with severe dyslexia and on a Beginning Reader level, struggled with sight words. As the rest of his class became more comfortable reading Shakespeare's words, he remained unsure. Could he read and understand Shakespeare? But he can't read! But he has a learning disability! But . . . nothing! Martin found his voice and his courage to try to read, and read he did. One day we were using the Folger Essential 3D Shakespeare to explore a scene, and when his turn came to read, he chose not to pass. Previously, he always politely declined to read aloud, and the class and I obliged. On this day, though, he did not pass. Slowly, he began to read the words. Fumbling often, he kept reading, with the encouragement and support of his peers. They helped him sound out words when he didn't know how to start. He finished reading, and the room applauded him. Martin entered center stage that day because he had developed both belief in himself and trust in his peers. He wanted to join them and believed he could do it. Shakespeare is truly for everyone, and everyone is capable of "getting it." Martin "got it," not because he read the text flawlessly and was able to analyze the motifs in an essay. He got it because he was able to understand the text through a series of activities that led to his comprehension.

Shakespeare and other excellent complex texts are so important, especially for students who have IEPs, because they deserve an enriching learning experience with real, challenging content. Giving students access to appropriate, grade-level material is essential to meeting their IEP goals, regardless of the educational setting (resource, pull-out, or inclusion). More than teaching Shakespeare, the Folger Method is also about instilling confidence in the students about the reality that they can do much of this work themselves. Even if it takes a while, even if they need a little help here and there—they can do it.

My Students and *Othello*

Connecting the Play to Their Own Lives

In general, multiple connections to any text build interest and improve comprehension. I have found that when my students connect elements of Shakespeare's plays to their own lives, they become more engaged in what they read and build stronger bonds to the text. In my classes, through the Folger approach, we have been building a safe, trusting community all along that makes it possible to explore these big ideas in the text.

Othello offers students any number of connections to their own lives. Here are a few, and ways in which you might use these in class:

Manipulation/Influence. Iago is able to control Othello and his actions through small steps of trust and loyalty. Bit by bit, Iago works to build Othello's trust in him, and he then manipulates that trust to influence Othello to murder Desdemona. There is a fine line between influence and manipulation, which comes from the intent of the action.

Idea for class: Before starting the play, students can engage in a physical anticipation guide. You can ask them opinion questions about the themes or actions in the text before reading it. Have students stand in a straight line facing one direction. For each statement you say, if students agree with it they can step forward; if they disagree, they will step backward. (You may need to move into a hallway or larger space depending on the size of the class.) Ideal statements to use are: It is important to help a friend make the right decisions; you should always trust your friend; your friends are more trustworthy than your romantic partner; sometimes people lie and that is okay; it doesn't matter how you do things, what matter is that they are done; the end goal is all that matters; only look out for yourself; people who are manipulated are weak; people cannot be trusted; etc. Students can then reflect on the questions and where they are standing when done.

Jealousy. Jealousy in the play is the catalyst behind Iago's plan and also the tool he uses to cause Othello to murder Desdemona. There are several causes of this jealousy: Othello's acclaim? Cassio's promotion? Racism? More? Iago is driven to extreme lengths to rid himself of Othello and then take his position. Jealousy is also what Iago uses to fuel his plan to manipulate Othello to murder Desdemona. Othello operates under blind jealousy when he murders Desdemona and refuses to reason with her.

Idea for class: Students can engage in the mindsets of the characters and events in the play by role-playing on a talk show analyzing Iago's and Othello's jealousy. An interesting third guest could be Emilia who we learn by the end of the play has a different perspective. First, the class will need to come up with a set of questions a talk show host should ask each character (as a teacher, you can also start with a few to help guide what a good question looks like). Next, students can work together to craft answers to these questions from the point of view of either Iago or Othello and find evidence in the text. Last, the class can stage the talk show by assigning a host to ask the questions and volunteers to be Iago, Othello, and Emilia answering the questions using their work.

Abusive Relationships. Desdemona in her final scene of the play attempts to persuade Othello to stop but does nothing physically to stop him. She simply surrenders to reality, counter to the opinions of others as to what she should have done. Desdemona has become the victim of an abusive relationship, created in part by Iago. The relationship did not start like this, and most abusive relationships do not.

Idea for class: Students can track the evolution of Othello and Desdemona's relationship on a timeline. By just focusing on their relationship, what happens to it, and at what times, students will find evidence from the text at each relationship point (i.e., when Othello comes home, how does Desdemona feel? How do you know? When Othello sees the handkerchief, what does he do or think? How do you know?). Using this timeline of their relationship, students can see how Iago creates the small mistrusts that build into the tragic ending.

Focus on Key Scenes

The lessons in this book focus on key scenes and use the Folger Essentials to actively and immediately involve students. The choice of key scenes is up to you. My students have had success focused on the following scenes: Othello and Desdemona's stories of their love, warnings, and Iago's speech (Act 1, scene 3); Iago's speech of revenge (Act 2, scene 1); Cassio's downfall and Iago's advice (Act 2, scene 3); Iago's seeds of jealousy (Act 3, scene 3); Othello confronts Desdemona (Act 3, scene 4); Othello and Iago's plans (Act 4, scene 1); Othello murders Desdemona (Act 5, scene 2).

I focus on key scenes and pay attention to these important guidelines:

Prioritize depth over breadth. It is more important that students learn the skills to dig deep into a text, especially independently, than it is to read every line in the play. It may take your class of students with IEPs the same amount of time to analyze 4 key scenes as it takes your general education class to analyze 7. That's okay. Give your students the time they need to do this important work rather than rush through the text. The scripts we create and use in class are without footnotes or explanatory glosses. This allows students to decipher meaning on their own or collaboratively and removes distractions that impede their understanding.

Keep the original language. Always use Shakespeare's original language and not the modernized, made-easy versions. Do not substitute simplified language to make it easier. For one thing, it doesn't make it easier. More importantly, students with IEPs need to be given access to the real thing—the original language—and be able to make sense of it. Because they can.

Shorten the scenes if you need to. You can cut key scenes to include just the most important information. Don't worry about cutting Shakespeare. For as long as Shakespeare's plays have been performed, they have been cut by directors and editors. To guide you, ask yourself these questions: What do I want students to understand from this scene? In what part of the scene does that idea happen? Below is a cut version of 1.3 that I used in my class.

The cut version of *Othello* 2.1 below is about 80 lines; the original scene is 334 lines. You can find the full text here: folger.edu/Othello/read, and you can download it for your own editing. Because the scene is brief, students can focus on meaning, setting, and characters on their own without getting lost. The cutting keeps the most important parts of plot and character. Using Folger Shakespeare online makes finding and cutting scenes easy.

DESDEMONA I thank you, valiant Cassio.
What tidings can you tell of my lord?

CASSIO
He is not yet arrived, nor know I aught
But that he's well and will be shortly here.
> *Within "A sail, a sail!" A shot.*

SECOND GENTLEMAN
They give their greeting to the citadel.

CASSIO See for the news.   *Second Gentleman exits.*
Good ancient, you are welcome. Welcome, mistress.
> *He kisses Emilia.*

IAGO Come on, come on! You are pictures out of door,
Players in your huswifery, and huswives in your beds.

DESDEMONA O heavy ignorance! Thou praisest the
worst best. But what praise couldst thou bestow on
a deserving woman indeed, one that in the authority
of her merit did justly put on the vouch of very
malice itself?

IAGO
She that was ever fair and never proud,
Had tongue at will and yet was never loud,
She that could think and ne'er disclose her mind,
See suitors following and not look behind,
She was a wight, if ever such wight were—

DESDEMONA To do what?

IAGO
To suckle fools and chronicle small beer.

DESDEMONA O, most lame and impotent conclusion!
How say you, Cassio? Is he not a most
profane and liberal counselor?

CASSIO He speaks home, madam.

Cassio takes Desdemona's hand.

IAGO, *aside* He takes her by the palm.
Ay, smile upon her, do. I will
gyve thee in thine own courtship.
If such tricks as these strip you out of
your lieutenantry. Yet
again your fingers to your lips? Would they were
clyster pipes for your sake!   *Trumpets within.*
The Moor. I know his trumpet.

CASSIO 'Tis truly so.

DESDEMONA Let's meet him and receive him.

CASSIO Lo, where he comes!

Enter Othello and Attendants.

OTHELLO
O, my fair warrior!

DESDEMONA My dear Othello!

OTHELLO
I cannot speak enough of this content.
It stops me here; it is too much of joy.   *They kiss.*

IAGO, *aside* O, you are well tuned now,
But I'll set down the pegs that make this music,
As honest as I am.

OTHELLO Come. Let us to the castle.—
News, friends! Our wars are done. The Turks are
drowned.
Come, Desdemona.
Once more, well met at Cyprus.

All but Iago and Roderigo exit.

IAGO, *to a departing Attendant* Do thou meet me presently
at the harbor. *To Roderigo.* Come hither. If
thou be'st valiant—
First, I must tell thee
this: Desdemona is directly in love with him.

RODERIGO With him? Why, 'tis not possible.

IAGO Lay thy finger thus, and let thy soul be instructed.
Mark me with what violence she first loved the
Moor but for bragging and telling her fantastical
lies. And will she love him still for prating? Let not
thy discreet heart think it. Her eye must be fed.
Now, sir,
this granted—as it is a most pregnant and unforced
position—who stands so eminent in the degree of
this fortune as Cassio does?

RODERIGO I cannot believe that in her. She's full of
most blessed condition.

IAGO Blessed fig's end! The wine she drinks is made of
grapes. If she had been blessed, she would never
have loved the Moor.

He exits.

IAGO
That Cassio loves her, I do well believe 't.
That she loves him, 'tis apt and of great credit.
The Moor, howbeit that I endure him not,
And nothing can or shall content my soul
Till I am evened with him, wife for wife,
Or, failing so, yet that I put the Moor
At least into a jealousy so strong
That judgment cannot cure.
I'll have our Michael Cassio on the hip,
Abuse him to the Moor in the rank garb
Make the Moor thank me, love me, and reward me
For making him egregiously an ass
Even to madness. 'Tis here, but yet confused.
Knavery's plain face is never seen till used.

He exits.

Annotating the Text

When I say "annotate," I mean making any notes about what is happening in the text; this practice helps students remember what is happening. Some may call this "marking the text." It's all the same. Encourage students to take notes directly on the text during discussions because it leads them to analysis.

Make it purposeful. Ensure that each time students annotate, they relate the underlined parts of the text to what is happening in the discussion. The annotations can be used for writing assignments.

Show them what an annotated scene or speech looks like and how it's useful. Model for students by annotating and thinking aloud with them. You can do this by using a projector or smartboard, or by distributing copies of your own annotations. The example below is a student's annotation of Act 5, scene 2.

Act 5, Scene 2

Enter Othello with a light, and Desdemona in her bed.

OTHELLO
It is the cause. Yet I'll not shed her blood, — refers to the end
Nor scar that whiter skin of hers than snow,
Yet she must die, else she'll betray more men.
Put out the light, and then put out the light.
I can again thy former light restore
Should I repent me. But once put out thy light,
Thou cunning'st pattern of excelling nature,
Justice to break her sword! *He kisses her* One
    more, one more.
Be thus when thou art dead, and I will kill thee   He is going to kill her!
And love thee after. One more, and this the last.

So sweet was ne'er so fatal. I must weep,   — why is he crying if he
But they are cruel tears. This sorrow's heavenly: is going to kill her?
It strikes where it doth love. She wakes.

He kisses her.
2x kisses her

DESDEMONA
Who's there? Othello?
OTHELLO Ay, Desdemona.
DESDEMONA Will you come to bed, my lord?
OTHELLO
Have you prayed tonight, Desdemon?
DESDEMONA Ay, my lord.
OTHELLO
Well, do it, and be brief. I will walk by.
I would not kill thy unprepared spirit.
DESDEMONA Talk you of killing? — is she upset? Tired? That's all she says?
OTHELLO
Ay, I do.
DESDEMONA
If you say so, I hope you will not kill me.   why doesn't she fight him?
OTHELLO Humh.
DESDEMONA
That death's unnatural that kills for loving.
Alas, why gnaw you so your nether lip?
Some bloody passion shakes your very frame.
OTHELLO Peace, and be still.   She asks how he is, concerned
DESDEMONA   more about him
I will so. What's the matter?
OTHELLO That handkerchief
Which I so loved, and gave thee, thou gav'st to
    Cassio.
DESDEMONA
No, by my life and soul! Send for the man
And ask him.

OTHELLO
 Sweet soul, take heed, take heed of perjury.
DESDEMONA
 Ay, but not yet to die.
OTHELLO Yes, presently.
 Therefore confess thee freely of thy sin.
 Thou art to die.
DESDEMONA
 And have you mercy, too. I never did
 Offend you in my life, never loved Cassio
 But with such general warranty of heaven
 As I might love. I never gave him token.
OTHELLO
 By heaven, I saw my handkerchief in 's hand!
 I saw the handkerchief!

Othello cannot be convinced. He's made up his mind already.

DESDEMONA He found it, then.
 Let him confess a truth.
OTHELLO He hath confessed.
DESDEMONA What, my lord?
OTHELLO
 That he hath used thee.
DESDEMONA How? Unlawfully?
OTHELLO Ay.
DESDEMONA
 He will not say so.
OTHELLO No. His mouth is stopped.
DESDEMONA
 O, my fear interprets. What, is he dead?
OTHELLO
 Had all his hairs been lives, my great revenge

— Cassio has been killed too!

DESDEMONA
 Alas, he is betrayed, and I undone.   *She weeps.*
OTHELLO
 Out, strumpet! Weep'st thou for him to my face?   *Unfaithful woman*
DESDEMONA
 O banish me, my lord, but kill me not!
OTHELLO Down, strumpet!
DESDEMONA
 Kill me tomorrow, let me live tonight.
OTHELLO Nay, if you strive—
DESDEMONA
 But half an hour!
OTHELLO Being done, there is no pause.   *— he has made up his mind.*
DESDEMONA
 But while I say one prayer!
OTHELLO It is too late.

                                        He smothers her.
                                        So there's no blood.

Spread the Shakespeare Love

You and your students are on a Shakespeare journey together. As with everything you teach, the energy you give is the energy you get back. The more you LOVE teaching Shakespeare, the more your students will love it too. Keep in mind that it may take time, so fake it until you make it. When I started using the Folger Method, my students thought I was way too excited about Shakespeare. Over time, the energy is contagious, and they are just as excited to learn as I am to teach. Shakespeare has always been my favorite unit because it demonstrates that powerful literature belongs to them, and my students look forward to it because it is fun. From calling each other "greasy onion-eyed nut-hook" and "rank rump-fed giglet" to fake swordplay and adding "thee" and "thou" to those words, I can see through their actions that they have fallen for Shakespeare as well.

Starting this journey with your students isn't always easy, but it is worth it. You are expecting more from them and teaching them more. Believe they can do the work and they will start to believe in themselves. Forgive yourself if a day does not work out. We are all works in progress, and it may take some tweaking to find out what extra things your students may need. Teaching Shakespeare or any other complex text using the Folger Method may be an adjustment to the way you teach now, so the more you do it, the better you will get at it. Students will become the drivers of the classroom, so get yourself ready for the show.

So, to my students who pop in to ask, "Hey, Ms. DiGenno, you still doing that Shakespeare thing?" "Yes, I am and so are you," I always say back as they rush out of the class again. Usually their last word: "Cool!"

Pairing Texts: *Othello* Off the Pedestal and in Conversation with Other Voices

Donna Denizé

Something wildly important happens when we teach two very different works or authors together—like *Macbeth* and the writings of Frederick Douglass; *Hamlet* and something by Claudia Rankine; *Othello* and poetry of George Moses Horton, or *The Taming of the Shrew* and the poems of Audre Lorde.

Paired texts are two texts that you and your students dive into at the same time. Both texts have equal weight; each is strong and can stand fully on its own. You can pair whole works or segments of works, selected narratives, scenes, or stanzas. But there is no "primary" and "secondary" or "supplemental" hierarchy—ever. Two voices, two points of view, two writing styles, two characters . . . and each will illuminate the other.

It's important to note here, since we are in the world of Shakespeare, that a Shakespeare play and an adaptation of a Shakespeare play or plot are not paired texts. That's a primary text and most often some kind of supplemental one. Together, they don't have the power or the payoff of a set of paired texts.

Why pair texts? Because, taken together, they illuminate each other in powerful and surprising ways. Looking closely at paired works gives kids a sense of the sweep of literature and allows them to consider together two authors who wrote in vastly different times, places, cultures, genders, races, religions—you name it. These juxtapositions allow them to notice that in many cases, writers have been asking the same big questions for some time: about human identity—how we define ourselves through culture, our moral choices, or how we navigate power or powerlessness, and more. In other instances, they are on very different wavelengths and . . . what might be the reasons for that?

I developed my love for paired texts in my thirty-eight years teaching in a variety of secondary school settings—public, private, urban, and rural—and in serving a term on the advisory board for all vocational schools in the state of Virginia. I currently teach at St. Albans School for Boys in Washington, DC, where I chair the English department. I love working with paired texts because two strong texts working together produce something marvelous in class: they create a space for meaningful conversations that come from students' experiences and questions, and this creates not just good analysis but empathy. Since students today must navigate an incredibly complex global society, they can only benefit by considering a sweep of literature that helps them deepen their empathy for others. I've found that the more specific or particular the pairing, the better, since this inspires students' creativity and establishes new ways of thinking about both texts. It also strengthens students' analytical skills and increases their capacity for understanding complexity—qualities that are essential for navigating current human challenges and the promise of an ever-evolving world—and the worlds students inhabit.

The following section is designed in two parts: Part One lays out an example of a pair of texts absent *Othello*—so that you can begin to get a sense of how paired texts work with each other, and how they work in class. In Part Two, I dive deeply into two *Othello* text pairs that have worked very successfully with my students.

Part One—The Example:
One Text Pair and How It All Went Down in Class—
Macbeth and Frederick Douglass's *Narrative*

1. Pairing *Macbeth's* **"If it were done" soliloquy** (1.7.1–28, Macbeth weighs plans to murder King Duncan) with the passage from **Frederick Douglass's *Narrative of the Life of Frederick Douglass: An American Slave***, in which Douglass sits on a hillside watching freely moving passing ships while his movement is confined by slavery, its laws, and its customs.

Macbeth 1.7.1–28 *by William Shakespeare*	Narrative of the Life of Frederick Douglass *by Frederick Douglass*
MACBETH If it were done when 'tis done, then 'twere well It were done quickly. If th' assassination Could trammel up the consequence and catch With his surcease success, that but this blow Might be the be-all and the end-all here, But here, upon this bank and shoal of time, We'd jump the life to come. But in these cases We still have judgment here, that we but teach Bloody instructions, which, being taught, return To plague th' inventor. This even-handed justice Commends th' ingredience of our poisoned chalice To our own lips. He's here in double trust: First, as I am his kinsman and his subject, Strong both against the deed; then, as his host, Who should against his murderer shut the door, Not bear the knife myself. Besides, this Duncan Hath borne his faculties so meek, hath been So clear in his great office, that his virtues Will plead like angels, trumpet-tongued, against The deep damnation of his taking-off;	Our house stood within a few rods of the Chesapeake Bay, whose broad bosom was ever white with sails from every quarter of the habitable globe. Those beautiful vessels, robed in purest white, so delightful to the eye of freemen, were to me so many shrouded ghosts, to terrify and torment me with thoughts of my wretched condition. I have often, in the deep stillness of a summer's Sabbath, stood all alone upon the lofty banks of that noble bay, and traced, with saddened heart and tearful eye, the countless number of sails moving off to the mighty ocean. The sight of these always affected me powerfully. My thoughts would compel utterance; and there, with no audience but the Almighty, I would pour out my soul's complaint, in my rude way, with an apostrophe to the moving multitude of ships:— "You are loosed from your moorings, and are free; I am fast in my chains, and am a slave! You move merrily before the gentle gale, and I sadly before the bloody whip! You are

And pity, like a naked newborn babe
Striding the blast, or heaven's cherubin horsed
Upon the sightless couriers of the air,
Shall blow the horrid deed in every eye,
That tears shall drown the wind. I have no spur
To prick the sides of my intent, but only
Vaulting ambition, which o'erleaps itself
And falls on th' other—

freedom's swift-winged angels, that fly round the world; I am confined in bands of iron! O that I were free! O, that I were on one of your gallant decks, and under your protecting wing! Alas! betwixt me and you, the turbid waters roll. Go on, go on. O that I could also go! Could I but swim! If I could fly! O, why was I born a man, of whom to make a brute. The glad ship is gone; she hides in the dim distance. I am left in the hottest hell of unending slavery. O God, save me! God, deliver me! Let me be free! Is there any God? Why am I a slave? I will run away. I will not stand it. Get caught, or get clear, I'll try it. I had as well die with ague as the fever. I have only one life to lose. I had as well be killed running as die standing. Only think of it; one hundred miles straight north, and I am free! Try it? Yes! God helping me, I will. It cannot be that I shall live and die a slave. I will take to the water. This very bay shall yet bear me into freedom. The steamboats steered in a north-east course from North Point. I will do the same; and when I get to the head of the bay, I will turn my canoe adrift, and walk straight through Delaware into Pennsylvania. When I get there, I shall not be required to have a pass; I can travel without being disturbed. Let but the first opportunity offer, and, come what will, I am off. Meanwhile, I will try to bear up under the yoke. I am not the only slave in the world. Why should I fret? I can bear as much as any of them. Besides, I am but a boy, and all boys are bound to some one. It may be that my misery in slavery will only increase my happiness when I get free. There is a better day coming."

Thus I used to think, and thus I used to speak to myself; goaded almost to madness at one moment, and at the next reconciling myself to my wretched lot.

In class, we started with a definition of ambition: Kids looked it up in various dictionaries. They came up with definitions like these:

- an earnest desire for some type of achievement or distinction, such as power, honor, fame, or wealth, and the willingness to strive for its attainment

- the object, state, or result desired or sought after

- to seek after earnestly

- to aspire to

I asked a few simple questions to start them off:

1. What is the ambition of each man? What is it driving him toward? What is he seeking?

2. What are they both wrestling against and with—morally and socially?

3. What solutions, if any, does each one reach?

A discussion developed that connected the word "ambition" with some of the other topics that they found in both texts: isolation; self-perception; moral dilemmas; questions about freedom and justice.

My students came up with valuable comparisons and contrasts that I list here in no particular order:

- Both are wrestling in the mind, the imagination alive, the struggle with consequences, moral right and wrong.

- In *Macbeth*, the moral wrong is in the individual; in the Douglass narrative, the moral wrong is in the larger society.

- Both bring isolation, pain, and suffering: Macbeth's isolation leads to his destruction; Douglass's isolation leads him to being an orator and a major voice in the cause for the abolition of slavery.

- Macbeth's ambition has a negative outcome, while Douglass's has a positive outcome.

- Both search for justice—Macbeth to avoid it and Douglass to have justice manifest.

- Macbeth has social and political power, while Douglass—a slave—is marginalized, without social and political power.

- Both are seeking freedom. Macbeth imagines freedom from consequences. Douglass imagines the consequences of freedom.

These two texts—Shakespeare's *Macbeth* and Frederick Douglass's *Narrative of the Life of Frederick Douglass: An American Slave*—are separated by time, space, culture, and geopolitics—and yet my students made wonderful connections between them, identifying isolation, self-perception, and moral dilemmas. They also asked big questions about freedom and justice, the function of human imagination, and ambition.

Part Two—*Othello:*
Two Text Pairs and How They Worked in Class

1. Pairing *Othello*'s **"This fellow's of exceeding honesty . . . Haply for I am black" soliloquy** (3.3.299–313), as Othello begins to question his wife's fidelity, his blackness, and begins to see his identity as "other," with **Derek Wolcott's poem "A Far Cry from Africa,"** in which the speaker feels tied to the cultural heritage of Africa but also loves the English language and literary tradition.

Othello *3.3.299–313* *by William Shakespeare*	*"A Far Cry from Africa"* *by Derek Wolcott*
OTHELLO This fellow's of exceeding honesty, And knows all qualities with a learnèd spirit Of human dealings. If I do prove her haggard, Though that her jesses were my dear heartstrings, I'd whistle her off and let her down the wind To prey at fortune. Haply, for I am black And have not those soft parts of conversation That chamberers have, or for I am declined Into the vale of years—yet that's not much— She's gone, I am abused, and my relief Must be to loathe her. O curse of marriage, That we can call these delicate creatures ours And not their appetites! I had rather be a toad And live upon the vapor of a dungeon Than keep a corner in the thing I love For others' uses.	A wind is ruffling the tawny pelt Of Africa. Kikuyu, quick as flies, Batten upon the bloodstreams of the veldt. Corpses are scattered through a paradise. Only the worm, colonel of carrion, cries: "Waste no compassion on these separate dead!" Statistics justify and scholars seize The salients of colonial policy. What is that to the white child hacked in bed? To savages, expendable as Jews? Threshed out by beaters, the long rushes break In a white dust of ibises whose cries Have wheeled since civilization's dawn From the parched river or beast-teeming plain. The violence of beast on beast is read As natural law, but upright man Seeks his divinity by inflicting pain. Delirious as these worried beasts, his wars Dance to the tightened carcass of a drum, While he calls courage still that native dread Of the white peace contracted by the dead. Again brutish necessity wipes its hands Upon the napkin of a dirty cause, again A waste of our compassion, as with Spain, The gorilla wrestles with the superman. I who am poisoned with the blood of both, Where shall I turn, divided to the vein? I who have cursed The drunken officer of British rule, how choose Between this Africa and the English tongue I love? Betray them both, or give back what they give? How can I face such slaughter and be cool? How can I turn from Africa and live?

First, we read both of these texts in class—aloud and chorally—so students have a sense of each both in terms of meaning and the cadence of the language. We don't talk about them, just read them. Then . . .

Since most students have several identifiers, we began the class with thinking about defining identity. I asked them to look up some dictionary definitions, which resulted in the following:

- Who you are, the way you think about yourself, the way you are viewed by the world, and the characteristics that define you

- The awareness that an individual or group has of being a distinct, persistent entity; the condition of being affiliated or associated with a group

- The appearance or mask one presents to the world, by which one is known

- The fact or condition of being associated or affiliated with something else

Using these definitions and specific language from the play, I asked students to find examples in which *Othello* is identified by others in the play's opening:

- Iago and Roderigo make numerous derogatory references to Othello's blackness and to his African heritage in the opening scene of the play: "thick lips," "old black ram," "devil," "gross clasps," "knave," and "lascivious."

- Brabantio: "such a thing as thou, to fear, not to delight (**1.2.90**)

- And again Brabantio: "For nature so prepost'rously to err / Being not deficient, blind, or lame of sense (**1.3.75–76**)

I then asked them to offer their own observations about how these others identify Othello at the play's opening. They came up with these:

- All of the identifiers are superficial, only related to skin color and stereotypes about blackness and/or Africans.

- Roderigo is prejudiced; he uses negative "racial" comments in reference to Othello because he, Roderigo, has an interest in Desdemona.

- Fear of the unknown, fear of the "other," seems to lead to violence in language, and if the fear remains unexamined, it leads to physical conflict and violence.

- Brabantio fears a romantic union between his daughter and the Black Othello.

- They mentioned that later, when it becomes clear that Brabantio had "lov'd" and "oft invited" Othello to his home to hear Othello's stories, Brabantio's double standard is revealed: Othello could be an exotic guest in Brabantio's home, but not a son-in-law.

Next, I asked students to choose a definition of "identity" and use it to clarify how Othello sees himself in the play's beginning. They had several answers:

- General/soldier; a morally virtuous person; a comrade in arms; an African; a mercenary, and a loving husband

Finally, I asked them to consider Othello and the speaker in Wolcott's poem. They spent some time considering, sometimes in small groups. The results were startling:

- Both Othello and Wolcott's speaker are caught between two worlds: European and African.

- Both have African roots, but they no longer speak a native tongue. They both experience an in-between-ness in their connection to English. Wolcott's speaker is a consummate poet and Othello is a consummate storyteller, but their mastery of powerful speech is accompanied—though for different reasons—by isolation and, in a sense, homelessness.

- They both have moral dilemmas, choices that are equally undesirable. Wolcott says he cannot betray the connection to his "English tongue," a consequence of British rule in St. Lucia. He also cannot betray his "blood" and the blood of Africans who were slaughtered through colonization.

- Othello's moral dilemma is connected to marriage. As a husband, Othello is divided between love for the wife he won through his stories and what he sees as his honor/duty: to uphold a moral code of marital fidelity and manhood, "else she'll betray more men" (**5.2.6**). Othello's moral dilemma or in-between-ness is connected not only to his land of origin, but also to marriage.

- In *Othello* and Wolcott's poem, both face prejudices that violate their individual identity.

Students also noted key differences:

- Othello condemns blackness and feels his blackness is now "base," making him uncultured and unlettered according to European standards; by contrast, Othello earlier had affirmed his African heritage ("I fetch my life and being/From men of royal siege," **1.2.24–25**). It feels like he begins to lose his identity as a general and a soldier, and as a husband, and says he'd rather be a "toad" and live in a dungeon than stay married to an unfaithful wife.

- Wolcott's speaker has no self-derogatory comment about blackness; rather, he is conscious of his in-between-ness, and openly states his inability to resolve the identity dilemma: he owes his identity to both Europe and Africa.

- Prejudice is a preconceived opinion that isn't based on reason or actual experience, so it leads to dangerous contradictions, violence, and blindness to the human connection with others. Brabantio's attitude also reveals the irrationality of prejudice.

- Because he refuses to deny both sides of his heritage, Wolcott's speaker does not experience despair, but unease—the result of living *in between spaces*. Othello does experience despair, it seems, because colonial expansionism emphasized binary realities: good vs. bad; right vs. wrong; black vs. white; civilized vs. uncivilized/ infidel, etc.; as a result, Othello is confronting a structural problem in society.

2. Pairing **Emilia's speech, "Good gentlemen, let me have leave to speak"** (5.2.232–263), Emilia affirming her loyalty to Desdemona by revealing Iago's deceptions about the handkerchief, with Fay Chiang's poem "Anger, Culture's Primary Step," on the belief that cycles of anger caused by societal and cultural injustice are only broken by confronting the truth. Fay Chiang (1952–2017) was an American poet based in New York who championed Asian-American culture.

Othello (5.2.232–263) by William Shakespeare	"Anger, Culture's Primary Step" by Fay Chiang
EMILIA Good gentlemen, let me have leave to speak. 'Tis proper I obey him, but not now. Perchance, Iago, I will ne'er go home. OTHELLO O, O, O! *Othello falls on the bed.* EMILIA Nay, lay thee down, and roar! For thou hast killed the sweetest innocent That e'er did lift up eye. OTHELLO, *standing* O, she was foul!— I scarce did know you, uncle. There lies your niece, Whose breath indeed these hands have newly stopped. I know this act shows horrible and grim. . . . OTHELLO 'Tis pitiful. But yet Iago knows That she with Cassio hath the act of shame A thousand times committed. Cassio confessed it, And she did gratify his amorous works With that recognizance and pledge of love Which I first gave her. I saw it in his hand. It was a handkerchief, an antique token My father gave my mother. EMILIA O God! O heavenly God! IAGO Zounds, hold your peace! EMILIA 'Twill out, 'twill out. I peace? No, I will speak as liberal as the north. Let heaven and men and devils, let them all, All, all, cry shame against me, yet I'll speak.	Images of anger I am told, should be left alone: regrettable, shameful, dismissable we remain mute from birth witness with transfixed eyes reality and lives burning with anguish; forcing us to cry out of need these lives, these conditions exist are repeated in silent complicity from one generation to the next Instead: break pact, give vent and form Shout! till they become common knowledge to be dealt with.

To begin, we read both texts together as a class, and I ask for their observations on Emilia's outburst.

1. They wonder about when Emilia realizes that her silence about Iago's poor treatment of her made her complicit in his acts of betrayal and deceit. They also wonder about what prompts her to confront the truth:

- her husband's evils?

- her love for Desdemona and loyalty to truth?

- her own blindness to evil?

2. I ask about what might force Emilia to shout out the truth about Desdemona's chastity and marital fidelity to those assembled.

Students gave some insightful responses:

- Emilia is eager for Iago's attentions.

- Emilia is determined to shout out the truth about Desdemona's virtue to ensure that Desdemona's reputation is properly cleared.

Finally, students made connections between Chiang's poem and Emilia's deathbed revelations of truth:

- One must not be silent about wrongdoing.

- Anger about wrongs is not enough; if the truth of matters is to be exposed, we must speak out, confront, and then address wrongs with right actions.

- This led to a long discussion about situations in their own lives and in the world at large that demand the truth be told.

Like the other examples in this chapter, Shakespeare's *Othello* and Fay Chiang's "Anger, Culture's Primary Step" are separated by time, space, culture, and geopolitics—and yet taken together, my students were able to make surprising connections and ask big questions about unexamined customs and traditions, as well as the dangers of hypocrisy and double standards.

Like poetry, these texts tell a story through what is left unsaid. Section IX of Muriel Rukeyser's poem "The Speed of Darkness" resonates here:

Time comes into it.
Say it.   Say it.
The universe is made of stories,
not of atoms.

The texts speak to history, to a cultural history that includes both human struggle and the strength of the human spirit—whether they be stories of captivity, freedom, exile, or migration. And perhaps the more we understand the untold stories of history, the better we will understand the many stories of our students.

Sources

Chiang, Fay "Anger, Culture's Primary Step," from *7 Continents, 9 Lives*. YBK Publishers, 2010. New York.

Douglass, Frederick. *Narrative of the Life of Frederick Douglass: An American Slave.* New York: Penguin Books, 1968. Print. https://docsouth.unc.edu/neh/douglass/douglass.html

Walcott, Derek. "A Far Cry from Africa," from *In a Green Night*. Copyright © 1962 by Derek Walcott. Reprinted by permission of Farrar, Straus and Giroux. All Rights Reserved.

PART FOUR

Five More Resources for You

- *Folger Teaching*—**teaching.folger.edu**—The Folger's online universe for teachers! Search lesson plans, podcasts, videos, and other classroom resources. Connect with like-minded colleagues and experts. Access on-demand teacher workshops and participate in a range of live professional development opportunities from hour-long sessions to longer courses, all offering CEU credit. Complete access to *Folger Teaching* is one of many benefits of joining the Folger as a **Teacher Member**.

- *Folger Shakespeare* online—**shakespeare.folger.edu**—Shakespeare's complete works free and online, and all downloadable in various formats that are particularly useful for classroom teachers and students. The Folger texts are the most up-to-date available online; behind the scenes, they have been encoded to make the plays easy to read, search, and index. Also available here are audio clips of selected lines performed.

- *Folger Shakespeare* in print—Shakespeare's plays and sonnets in single-volume paperbacks and in ebooks. The texts are identical to those of *Folger Shakespeare* online; the books, however, are all in the format featuring the text on the right-hand page with glosses and definitions on the left. Used in many, many classrooms, the *Folger Shakespeare* in print is published by Simon & Schuster and available from booksellers everywhere.

- *The Folger Shakespeare Library*—**folger.edu**—The online home of the wide world of the Folger Shakespeare Library, offering all kinds of experiences and resources from the world's largest Shakespeare collection. Become a Folger researcher, join scholarly seminars, explore the Folger collection, enjoy the magic of theatre, music, and poetry, and prepare for a visit to the Folger. We're waiting for you, your class, and your family! An opportunity for deep, lively, and satisfying engagement with the humanities.

- *Shakespeare Documented*—**shakespearedocumented.folger.edu**—A singular site that brings together digitized versions of hundreds of the known primary-source documents pertaining to Shakespeare—the playwright, actor, and stakeholder; the poet, and the man engaged in family and legal matters. A destination for curious students! Convened by the Folger, this collection is a collaboration among the Folger and Shakespeare Birthplace Trust, the National Archives of Great Britain, the Bodleian Library at Oxford, and the British Library.

ACKNOWLEDGMENTS

Seven or eight years ago, Mark Miazga, an exceptional high school teacher from Baltimore—and a Folger teacher—said, "We should make a series of books where we lay out for teachers key specifics about the play, and then how to teach the whole play using the Folger Method."

Ignition.

An important idea with a huge scope: five books, each focused on a single play—*Hamlet, Macbeth, Romeo and Juliet, Othello,* and *A Midsummer Night's Dream.* Each one a pretty revolutionary dive into basic info, scholarship, and the how of teaching each of the plays to *all* students. *Every* student. This demanded assembling an extraordinarily strong array of knowledge, expertise, and experience and moving it into action.

It is finally time to name and celebrate this crowd of people who, with generosity of all kinds, had a hand in creating the book that you are reading right now:

Folger Director Michael Witmore, a deep believer in the importance of learning, teaching, and the power of the Folger to support both for all and at all levels, has been a fan and a wise advisor from the start.

The generosity of the Carol and Gene Ludwig Family Foundation—and in particular our fairy godmother, Carol Ludwig—has fueled every part of the creation of this series, including making certain that every English teacher in Washington, DC, has their own set of books *gratis.* I express the gratitude of the Folger as well as that of teachers in DC and beyond.

None of these volumes would exist without Folger Education's extraordinary Katie Dvorak, who, from the first minute to the last, herded not cats but our many authors, contracts, editorial conferences, publisher meetings, the general editor, and a series of deadlines that *never, ever* stopped changing. Much of this was accomplished as Covid covered all lives, work, families, everything. Katie's persistence, along with her grace, humor, empathy, and patience, kept us moving and was the glue we never did not need.

We appreciate the support and guidance of our team at Simon & Schuster: Irene Kheradi, Johanna Li, and Amanda Mulholland.

All along, the overall project benefited from the wisdom and support of these key players: Skip Nicholson, Heather Lester, Michael LoMonico, Corinne Viglietta, Maryam Trowell, Shanta Bryant, Missy Springsteen-Haupt, and Jessica Frazier . . . and from the creative genius of Mya Gosling.

Major gratitude to colleagues across the Folger who contributed to building these books in terms of both content and business support. Our thanks to Erin Blake, Caroline Duroselle-Melish, Beth Emelson, Abbey Fagan, Esther French, Eric Johnson, Adrienne Jones, Ruth Taylor Kidd, Melanie Leung, Mimi Newcastle, Rebecca Niles, Emma Poltrack, Sara Schliep, Emily Wall, and Heather Wolfe.

We are in debt to the schoolteachers and scholars who generously shared their time and wisdom as we got started, helping us to map our path and put it in motion—all along the intersections where scholarship and teaching practice inform each other. Massive gratitude to Patricia Akhimie, Bernadette Andreas, Ashley Bessicks, David Sterling Brown, Patricia Cahill, Jocelyn Chadwick, Eric DeBarros, Donna Denizé, Ambereen Dadabhoy, Ruben Espinosa, Kyle Grady, Kim Hall, Caleen Sinnette Jennings, Stefanie Jochman, Heather Lester, Catherine Loomis, Ellen McKay, Mark Miazga, Noémie Ndiaye, Gail Kern Paster, Amber Phelps, Katie Santos, Ian Smith, Christina Torres, and Jessica Cakrasenjaya Zeiss.

It's impossible to express our thanks here without a special shout-out to Ayanna Thompson, the scholarly powerhouse who has been nudging Folger Education for the last decade. Know that nudges from Ayanna are more like rockets . . . always carrying love and a challenge. We could not be more grateful for them, or for her.

Finally, and with endless admiration, we give the close-to-last words and thanks to the working schoolteachers who authored major portions of these books. First here, we honor our colleague Donnaye Moore, teacher at Brookwood High School in Snellville, Georgia, who started on this project teaching and writing about *Othello* but succumbed to cancer far too soon. None of us have stopped missing her or trying to emulate her brilliant practicality.

I asked working teachers to take on this challenge because I know that no one knows the "how" of teaching better than those who do it in classrooms every day. The marvels I am about to name were teaching and living through all the challenges that Covid presented in their own lives and thinking about you and your students too, putting together (and testing and revising) these lessons for you who will use these books. Over a really loud old-fashioned PA system, I am shouting the names of Ashley Bessicks, Noelle Cammon, Donna Denizé, Roni DiGenno, Liz Dixon, David Fulco, Deborah Gascon, Stefanie Jochman, Mark Miazga, Amber Phelps, Vidula Plante, Christina Porter, and Jessica Cakrasenjaya Zeiss! You rock in every way possible. You honor the Folger—and teachers everywhere—with your wisdom, industry, and generosity.

Finally, I wrap up this project with humility, massive gratitude to all for all, and—perhaps amazingly in the complicated days in which we are publishing—HOPE. Hamza, Nailah, and Shazia O'Brien, Soraya Margaret Banta, George and Brendan Mutrie, and gazillions of children in all parts of the world deserve all we've got. Literature—in school, even!—can get us talking to, and learning from, one another in peace. Let's get busy.

—Peggy O'Brien,
General Editor

ABOUT THE AUTHORS

Ambereen Dadabhoy completed her PhD in English Literature from Claremont Graduate University in 2008. She has taught at Boğaziçi University in Istanbul and is an Associate Professor of Literature at Harvey Mudd College in California. What both of those experiences share are intellectually curious students, stimulating environments, and challenging courses. Ambereen's teaching and research focus on early modern English literature, specifically drama and the representation of race and religion on the English stage. She is also passionately committed to social justice work inside and outside of the classroom and in higher education.

Catherine Loomis holds a PhD in Renaissance Literature from the University of Rochester and an MA in Shakespeare and Performance from the Shakespeare Institute. She is the author of *William Shakespeare: A Documentary Volume* (Gale, 2002) and *The Death of Elizabeth I: Remembering and Reconstructing the Virgin Queen* (Palgrave, 2010), and, with Sid Ray, the editor of *Shaping Shakespeare for Performance: The Bear Stage* (Fairleigh Dickinson, 2016). She has taught at the University of New Orleans, the University of North Carolina at Greensboro, and the Rochester Institute of Technology.

Christina Porter is a 2006 alum of the Teaching Shakespeare Institute at the Folger Shakespeare Library. Prior to her current position as Director of Humanities she was an English teacher and literacy coach for Revere Public Schools in Revere, Massachusetts. Dr. Porter is also a faculty member at Salem State University. She resides in Salem, Massachusetts, with her two precocious daughters.

Corinne Viglietta teaches Upper School English at The Bryn Mawr School in Baltimore, Maryland. From 2014 to 2022, Corinne was associate director of education at the Folger Shakespeare Library, where she had the honor of exploring the wonders of language with thousands of amazing teachers, students, and visitors. Corinne played a key role in growing Folger's national teaching community, school partnerships, and led numerous workshops on the Folger Method. She is a lifelong Folger educator, having first discovered the power of this approach with her multilingual stu-

dents in Washington, DC, and France. She has degrees in English from the University of Notre Dame and the University of Maryland.

David A. Fulco is a New York City–based educator. He works at the Laboratory School of Finance and Technology (HS223) in the South Bronx as an 11th/12th-grade English teacher and teacher leader. He is also the advisor to *The Eagle Express*, the student newspaper of HS223. David was a proud member of TSI 2014! He lives with his wife, Meaghan and his nine-year-old daughter, Annalena, who have been incredible supports to him throughout this process.

Of Haitian American descent, **Donna Denizé** holds a BA from Stonehill College and an MA in Renaissance Drama from Howard University, where she was also a student of poet Robert Hayden while he served as Consultant to the Library of Congress. She has contributed to scholarly books and journals, and she is the author of a chapbook, *The Lover's Voice* (1997), and a book, *Broken Like Job* (2005). She currently chairs the English Department at St. Albans School for boys, where she teaches Freshman English; a junior/senior elective in Shakespeare; and Crossroads in American Identity, a course she designed years ago and which affords her the opportunity to do what she most enjoys—exploring not only the cultural and inter-textual crossroads of literary works but also their points of human unity.

Heather Lester is a joyful 11th/12th-grade English teacher at International High School at LaGuardia Community College in Queens, New York. She began her career three decades ago as an intern for the Folger's Teaching Shakespeare Institute and returned to TSI in 2018 and 2021 as a mentor teacher. Before becoming a full-time New York City classroom teacher, she was a theater teaching artist, an arts program manager, and a writer for the Brooklyn Academy of Music, the Creative Arts Team, and the Center for Arts Education.

Jocelyn A. Chadwick is a lifelong English teacher and international scholar. She was a full-time professor at Harvard Graduate School of Education and now occasionally lectures and conducts seminars there. In addition to teaching and writing, Chadwick consults and works with teachers and elementary, middle, and high school students around the country. She has worked with PBS, BBC Radio, and NBC News Learn, and is a past president of the National Council of Teachers of English. Chadwick has written many articles and books, including *The Jim Dilemma: Reading Race in* Adventures of Huckleberry Finn, *Teaching Literature in the Context of Literacy Instruction*, and more. Chadwick is currently working on her next book, *Writing for Life: Using Literature to Teach Writing*.

Kim F. Hall is Lucyle Hook Professor of English and Professor of Africana Studies at Barnard College, where she teaches courses in Critical Race Studies, Black Feminist Studies, and material culture. Her book *Things of Darkness: Economies of Race and Gender in Early Modern England* helped create the field known as premodern critical race studies. She has written on the racialization of the archives and has taught and lectured widely on questions of race and culture to every-

one from Black sororities to middle and high school teachers to college communities. Additionally, she has taught art practices in programs for placed-at-risk students, quilt guilds, and senior centers. The Barnard College Library named her their first Faculty Partner of the Year, and she led the effort to acquire the Ntozake Shange Collection at Barnard, which has helped renew the college archive as a feminist space. *Diverse Issues in Higher Education* named her one of "25 Women Making a Difference in Higher Education and Beyond" largely on the basis of her "Digital Shange Project," in which undergraduates use digital tools and archival research to learn about Shange's work and legacy. She has won several prestigious fellowships, including a National Humanities Center Fellowship; a Fellowship at the Schomburg Center for Research in Black Culture; an NEH fellowship at the Newberry Library in Chicago; and an ACLS fellowship. HBCU and other Black archives play a large role in her current project, *Othello Was My Grandfather: Shakespeare and Race in the African Diaspora.*

Michael LoMonico has taught Shakespeare courses and workshops for teachers and students in 40 states as well as in Canada, England, and the Bahamas. He was an assistant to the editor for the curriculum section of all three volumes of the Folger's Shakespeare Set Free series. Until 2019, he was the Senior Consultant on National Education for the Folger. He is the author of *The Shakespeare Book of Lists, Shakespeare 101,* and a novel, *That Shakespeare Kid.* He was the co-founder and editor of *Shakespeare,* a magazine published by Cambridge University Press and Georgetown University.

Michael Witmore was the seventh director of the Folger Shakespeare Library, the world's largest Shakespeare collection and the ultimate resource for exploring Shakespeare and his world. He was appointed to this position in July 2011; prior to leading the Folger, he was professor of English at the University of Wisconsin-Madison and at Carnegie Mellon University. Under his leadership and across a range of programs and policies, the Folger began the process of opening up to and connecting with greater and more diverse audiences nationally, internationally, and here at home in Washington, DC. He believes deeply in the importance of teachers; also under his leadership, the Library's work in service of schoolteachers grew in breadth, depth, and accessibility.

Mya Lixian Gosling (she/her) is the artist and author of *Good Tickle Brain,* the world's foremost (and possibly only) stick-figure Shakespeare comic, which has been entertaining Shakespeare geeks around the world since 2013. Mya also draws *Keep Calm and Muslim On,* which she co-authors with Muslim-American friends, and *Sketchy Beta,* an autobiographical comic documenting her misadventures as an amateur rock climber. In her so-called spare time, Mya likes to read books on random Plantagenets, play the ukulele badly, and pretend to be one of those outdoorsy people who is in touch with nature but actually isn't. You can find her work at goodticklebrain.com.

With over 17 years in education, **Noelle Cammon** has cultivated a deep-seated love for English and an unwavering dedication to nurturing the minds of young learners. She is an alum of Teaching Shakespeare 2018. Since 2022, she has served as a distinguished Folger Fellow, collaborating with Folger Education and Reconstruction.us on the Black Shakespeare curriculum, aiming to bring diversity and inclusivity to the forefront of literary education. Noelle has a master's degree in English Literature from California Polytechnic University, Pomona. She currently teaches English at Heritage High School in Menifee, California.

Peggy O'Brien founded the Folger Shakespeare Library's Education Department in 1981. She set the Library's mission for K–12 students and teachers then and began to put it in motion; among a range of other programs, she founded and directed the Library's intensive Teaching Shakespeare Institute, was instigator and general editor of the popular Shakespeare Set Free series, and expanded the Library's education work across the country. In 1994, she took a short break from the Folger—twenty years—but returned to further expand the education work and to engage in opening up the Folger to many more people—including teachers. She is the instigator and general editor of the Folger Guides to Teaching Shakespeare series.

Roni DiGenno is a special education teacher at Calvin Coolidge Senior High School in Washington, DC. She earned her BA in Literature from Stockton University in Pomona, New Jersey, and her MA in English from Rutgers University in Camden, New Jersey. Her background in English and passion for special education led her to the educational mission of the Folger Shakespeare Library, participating in the Teaching Shakespeare Institute in 2016. She currently lives in Maryland with her husband, daughter, and two dogs.